Blue Line 5

Workbook

Ausgabe für Bayern (Mittelschulen R-Zug)

Herausgeber: Wolfgang Hamm

Ernst Klett Verlag GmbH
Stuttgart • Leipzig • Dortmund

Hör-Dateien online wz68ud

Around Australia

10/2

1 Read the blog posts and complete them. Choose one picture for each text.

G'day ✓ | Australians | Great Barrier Reef | online | Aboriginal | creatures | koala | outback | water | barbecue | School of the Air

INTERNET

G'day________ everyone!

Yesterday I saw one of the world's most beautiful sights, the ____________________. Thousands of different ____________________ live there, even sharks. We saw beautiful birds and fish. I can now understand why Australians love ________________ sports and the beach. In the afternoon we had a ____________________ and met some ____________________ people. They showed us a traditional dance which was amazing. Well, I'll tell you more next time.

See you soon,

Anne

Picture ☐

INTERNET

Hi everybody,

This is my third day in the ________________, the hot centre of Australia. Few ________________ live here. Guess what! There are no schools for children in the outback. Children have their school lessons ________________ at the ________________ ________________. There are lots of sheep and kangaroos but my favourite Australian animal is the ________________. Believe it or not, they sleep for 16 to 20 hours a day! But you can only see them in the south-east of the country.

Bye for today,

Sam

Picture ☐

1
11/3

2 (LISTENING) Listen to Peter's talk about the School of the Air. Tick.

1.	Where does Peter live?	a) in Alice Springs (c)	☐	b) on a sheep station (p)	☐
2.	How far away is the school?	a) 200 km (h)	☐	b) 2,000 km (a)	☐
3.	What is free for students?	a) a bus ticket (m)	☐	b) the IT equipment (o)	☐
4.	What does Peter miss?	a) the lunch break (i)	☐	b) team sports (n)	☐
5.	How often do the students meet?	a) three times a year (e)	☐	b) once a year (l)	☐

Take the letters at the end of your answers and complete the sentence:

Peter can always e-mail his teacher or ________________ him once a week.

12/2 1 Complete the crossword.

1. Food that you like very much is …
2. another word for a 'trip'
3. to look after someone or something
4. You can eat … meat in Australia.
5. a picture painted by an Aboriginal artist (2 words)
6. Aboriginal people play music on it.
7. another word for 'very big'
8. a group of Aboriginals who live together
9. a city on the west coast of Australia
10. the name of the big rock in the Australian outback

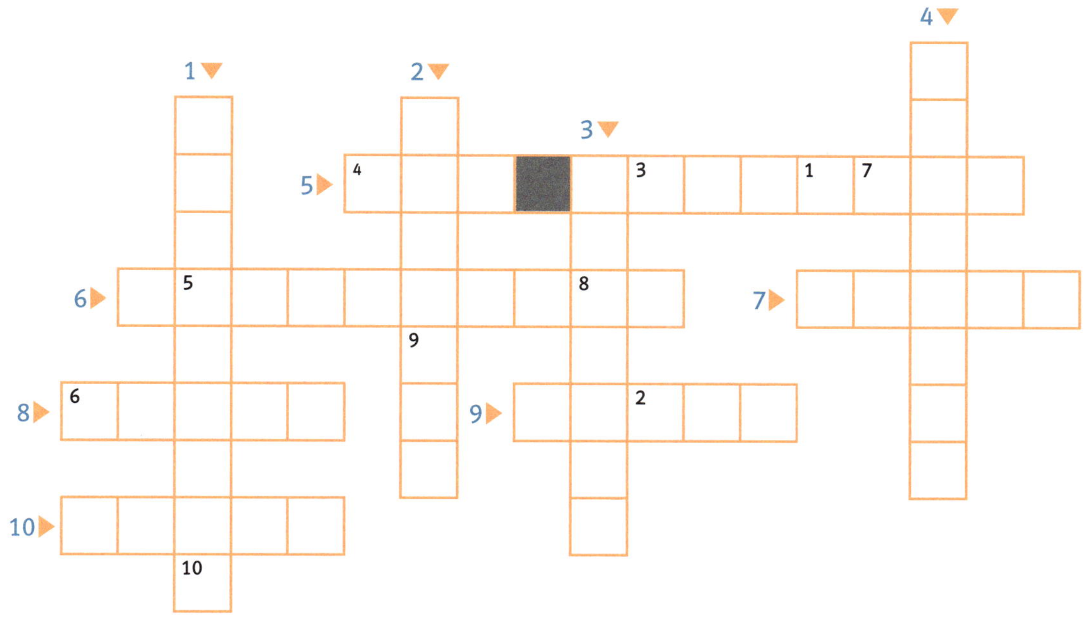

Complete the sentence with the right word.

The Aboriginal tribes have a lot of

1	2	3	4	5	6	7	8	9	10

13/4 2 Complete the blog post with the correct adjectives from the box. You don't need all the words.

afraid • big ✓ • clever • colourful • dark • delicious • disappointed • exciting • free • important • long • modern • surprised

INTERNET

Hi everyone!

I visited the (1) big ________ beautiful rock Uluru in the outback with my family yesterday. At first I was (2) ________ that you aren't allowed to climb the rock. You must know, Uluru is an (3) ________ place for the Aboriginal people. A guide took us on a (4) ________ walk (more than 3 hours!). We saw some very (5) ________ dot paintings. At the end of the day I was (6) ________ how (7) ________ it is in the outback at night. But I wasn't (8) ________. We sat around a fire and listened to some (9) ________ Aboriginal stories. It was great.

Bye for today, Bega

14/6 ## 3 Complete the text with the right form of the verbs in brackets. Use the simple past.

My name is Bega and my family are Aboriginal people. I (1) ____________ (not know) much about our traditions, so I (2) ____________ (ask) my grandma. She (3) ____________ (tell) me that a long time ago very big creatures (4) ____________ (come) and (5) ____________ (make) the landscape. When my family and I (6) ____________ (visit) Uluru we (7) ____________ (have) a great barbecue in the evening. There (8) ____________ (be) wonderful vegetables and lots of meat, but there (9) ____________ (not be) any fish. The food (10) ____________ (taste) delicious. However, my sister (11) ____________ (not like) it.

14/7 ## 4 (SPEAKING) The best holiday trip ever

a) Complete the questions. Use the simple past.

1. What ____________ you ____________ (see) in Italy?
2. ____________ you ____________ (visit) a gallery?
3. When ____________ you ____________ (come) home?
4. Where ____________ you ____________ (go) on holiday?
5. ____________ you ____________ (like) the paintings?
6. ____________ you ____________ (eat) lots of ice cream?
7. Where ____________ you ____________ (stay)?
8. What food ____________ you ____________ (like) most in Italy?

b) Find a question from a) for each answer in b) and write it down. Then act the dialogue.

Partner A	Partner B
1. ____________	We went to Italy.
2. ____________	We stayed at a nice campsite.
3. ____________	No, I don't like ice cream.
4. ____________	I saw a lot of churches and old buildings.
5. ____________	Yes, we went to a gallery in Pisa.
6. ____________	Yes, I liked some of the paintings.
7. ____________	I loved the pizzas.
8. ____________	We came home last Sunday.

c) Use the questions to act your own dialogue.

17/4

1 Useful phrases

a) Match a word from the left box with a word from the right box and write down the phrase next to its German meaning.

get well • drink • catch • take • have • stay • have • make	an appointment • tea • a cold • soon • a headache • in bed • tablets • a high temperature

1. Fieber haben ____ _ ____ ____________ (12th letter)
2. Kopfschmerzen haben ____ _ ________ (7th letter)
3. im Bett bleiben ____ __ ___ (9th letter)
4. Tee trinken _____ ___ (3rd letter)
5. eine Erkältung kriegen _____ _ ____ (1st letter)
6. einen Termin vereinbaren ____ __ ___________ (11th letter)
7. Gute Besserung! ___ ____ ____ (11th letter)
8. Tabletten nehmen ____ _______ (4th letter)

b) Take the letters from the right in a) and you'll get a new word:

1.	2.	3.	4.	5.	6.	7.	8.

17/5

2 (SPEAKING) At the doctor's

a) Read the dialogues and cross out the wrong words.

In the morning:

Receptionist: Hello, this is Braddon Doctors. How can I help you?

Patient: Hello. My name is Sarah Walton. I would like to make **an appointment.** • **a prescription.** I have a headache and **a high** • **a cold** temperature.

Receptionist: OK, you can come and **see** • **register** the doctor at 4:00 p.m. today.

In the afternoon:

Doctor: Hello Mrs Walton, how are you today?

Patient: Hello Doctor Miller. I don't feel very well. I have a headache and I **have** • **feel** hot.

Doctor: Well, let me see. OK, I think you've **found** • **caught** the flu. You'll have to stay in bed for a few days. Here's a **prescription** • **pharmacy** for some medicine. Take two **tablets** • **tables** every day, one in the morning and one in the evening.

Patient: Oh no. It's my birthday on Saturday.

Doctor: You'll be **fine** • **busy** by then. Don't worry. Goodbye and get well soon.

Patient: Thank you, Doctor Miller. Goodbye.

b) Act the dialogues with a partner.

2 17/6

3 (LISTENING) Listen to Dr Miller and four people with problems. Tick right or wrong. Underline the wrong words and correct them. Four sentences are true.

		right	wrong
1. Mrs Dawson forgot to take her tablets.	______	☐	☐
2. Dr Miller told her not to take yesterday's tablets.	______	☐	☐
3. Matt fell off his bike and broke his arm.	______	☐	☐
4. The doctor told Matt not to do any sport for a year.	______	☐	☐
5. Mrs Carter's daughter Jenny is crying.	______	☐	☐
6. Jenny is OK but her mother caught a cold.	______	☐	☐
7. Dr Miller gave Jenny a prescription for some medicine.	______	☐	☐
8. Brian Dickens has a high temperature and can't come to the doctor's at 3:30 p.m.	______	☐	☐

3 17/6

4 (SOUNDS) Say the words. How many syllables? Listen and check your answers.

1. pharmacy [3]
2. appointment ☐
3. prescription ☐
4. tablets ☐
5. headache ☐
6. tomorrow ☐
7. congratulations ☐
8. Australian ☐

18/7

5 Complete the sentences. Use the will-future.

1. If Chris goes to football practice, the flu ______ (get) worse.
2. His head ______ (not hurt) any more if he takes his medicine.
3. You ______ (be) OK if you stay in bed for two days.
4. If Sue stays in bed for the weekend, she ______ (feel) much better.
5. If you ask your friends, they ______ (send) you some pictures.
6. They ______ (not be) angry if you stay at home.
7. You ______ (sleep) much better if you take your medicine.
8. Mum ______ (take) you to the doctor's if you don't feel better tomorrow.

18/8

6 Choose the right verbs.

doesn't play | feels ✓ | wins | will get | will have | will play | can see | takes

1. If Chris *feels* ______ better next week, he ______ in the next football game.
2. If Chris ______ football this week, he ______ better soon.
3. If he ______ his medicine every day, he ______ his cousins at the weekend.
4. If he ______ the next game, he ______ a barbecue with his friends.

7 What will you do if …? Complete the sentences. You can choose from the pictures or use your own ideas.

19/10

stay … | order … | go to … | invite … | go …

1. If the weather is warm, I ______________________ with my dog.

2. If my parents are not at home on Friday night, I ______________________.

3. If we are hungry, we ______________________.

4. If it rains at the weekend, my friends and I ______________________.

5. If I feel tired, I ______________________.

8 Complete Dr Miller's advice.

19/10

1. If you want to get better soon, t _ _ _ this medicine.
2. Go to the pharmacy if you don't have the t _ _ _ _ _ _ at home.
3. If you stay in bed for the weekend, you can go to the b _ _ _ _ next week.
4. But if you still feel tired at the beach, then don't go into the w _ _ _ _.
5. Call us and make another appointment if you're not b _ _ _ _ _ by Monday.

9 (SPEAKING) Talk about being ill.

19/11

Partner A

Begrüße Partner B und frage, wie es ihm oder ihr geht.

Hello. How ______________________

Partner B

Sage, dass es dir nicht gut geht. Du hast schlimme Kopfschmerzen.

I don't feel well. I have a ______________________

Partner A

Sage, dass es dir Leid tut. Es gibt eine Apotheke um die Ecke. Dort kann Partner B Medizin kaufen.

Oh dear. There's a ______________________

____

____

Partner B

Du bist dir nicht sicher und sagst, dass du außerdem Fieber hast.

____

____

____

Partner A

Du denkst, dass Partner B dann lieber zum Arzt gehen sollte.

____

Partner B

Ja, Partner A hat wahrscheinlich recht. Du wirst einen Termin machen.

____

____

Partner A

Du wünschst gute Besserung.

____

Partner B

Du bedankst dich.

____

22/2 1 (MEDIATION) Pass on information at a pharmacy.

Finn aus Coburg ist mit seiner jüngeren Schwester Hanna, 12, bei Verwandten in Sydney zu Gast. Eines Morgens wacht Hanna mit starken Kopfschmerzen und Fieber auf. Sie gehen in eine Apotheke. Übernimm Finns Rolle und vermittle sinngemäß. Hier sind ein paar Hilfen.

How much ...? | bad headache | really hot | stay in bed | have to take

Pharmacist: G'day. Oh dear, what's the matter?

You: Der Apotheker fragt, was los ist. ____

Hanna: Als ich heute früh aufgewacht bin, hatte ich fürchterliche Kopfschmerzen und mir war heiß.

You: When she woke up this morning, she ____

Pharmacist: Oh, I think you've caught a cold then. A lot of people have one at the moment.

You: Er meint, dass du ____

Hanna: Muss ich im Bett bleiben?

You: Does she have to ____

Pharmacist: No, you don't. You should take these tablets. They'll help you.

You: Er sagt, ____

Hanna: Und wann muss ich sie nehmen?

You: When ____

Pharmacist: Take two tablets every day, one in the morning and one in the evening. Go to the doctor if you're not better by the beginning of next week.

You: ____

Hanna: OK. Was kosten denn die Tabletten?

You: ____

Pharmacist: 24 tablets are $11.99.

You: ____

Hanna: Alles klar, gibst du ihm das Geld bitte?

You: ____

Pharmacist: Thank you. Get well soon.

You: ____

Hanna: Thank you. Bye.

Fire at the sheep station

A It was in the middle of the night. I opened my eyes as my friend Rachel jumped out of bed and opened the door. And then there was this smell ...! Rachel and I shouted, "Fire!" We ran outside.

B In the outback it is often hot and windy, and the land is dry. This year it was even drier and hotter than the years before. We were scared. We could see the fire in the fields. I felt the wind. The fire came nearer.

C "OK, Sonya and Rachel," shouted Ally, the station manager. "Move the sheep into the fields behind the house." Then she shouted to the workers, "You! Put all the pets and chickens into the cages." It was difficult to move the sheep because they were very nervous. The wind got warmer around us. Rachel and I looked at each other. "This is getting scary," she said.
Finally we got all the sheep in. As we closed the gates, we heard the sound of helicopters. They were there to drop water on the fires. Some farm workers got things ready to leave the farm. "Are we leaving?" I asked Ally. "Maybe," she answered. "We're waiting for a decision."

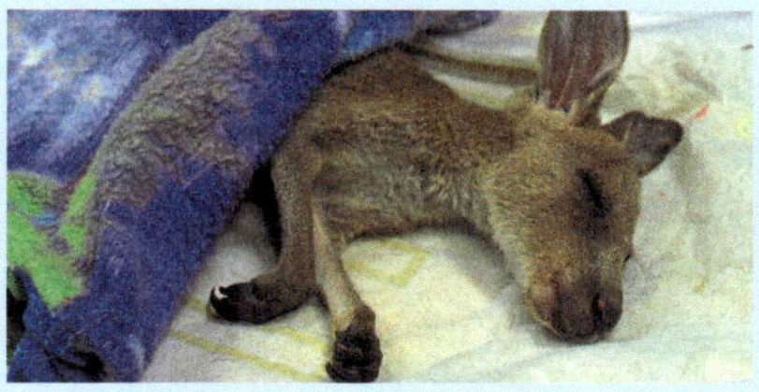

D Then a car stopped in front of us and some workers jumped out. One of them was holding something in her arms. "Can you take this?" she asked. I saw a baby kangaroo and took it from her. "It was on the road but I think it's OK," she said. "Some water would be good for it." "OK." I looked at the sweet little creature in my arms and couldn't believe my eyes. Then I got some water for my new friend.

E A little later Ally called, "Right everyone, good news. The wind has changed so we will stay here for now. A group of us must protect the house and the animals. The rest of us must check the fire doesn't start again." Rachel and I were happy in the end but also a little nervous as we looked at the orange and grey sky.

21/4 **1** (READING) **Read the text. Match the headings with the right parts (A–E) of the text. You don't need one of the headings.**

1. A sweet little surprise ☐
2. Getting up and out quickly ☐
3. Happy, but still checking for danger ☐
4. Scary fire in the fields ☐
5. Leaving the farm ☐
6. Plans for animal safety ☐

21/4 **2** **Read the questions. Complete the answers. These words can help.**

move the sheep | run outside | drop water | on the road | hot | dry

1. What did Sonya and Rachel do when they woke up? They ____________
2. Why are there often fires in the outback? Because it ____________ and the land ____________
3. What did Ally ask the girls to do? To ____________ behind the house.
4. Why were there helicopters? Because they ____________
5. Where did the workers find the baby kangaroo? ____________

Lösungen online
z53m6b

1. Löse alle Aufgaben.
2. Überprüfe deine Lösungen online. Gib dazu den Code in das Suchfeld auf der Klett-Homepage ein. Die Internetadresse findest du vorne im Heft.
3. Gib dir selbst Punkte. Wenn du weniger als die Hälfte der Punkte hast, übe auf den Step by step-Seiten (z. B. bei Unit 1 auf S. 12–13).

___/8P

Ziel 1: Ich kann Informationen über Australien verstehen.

→p. 12/1

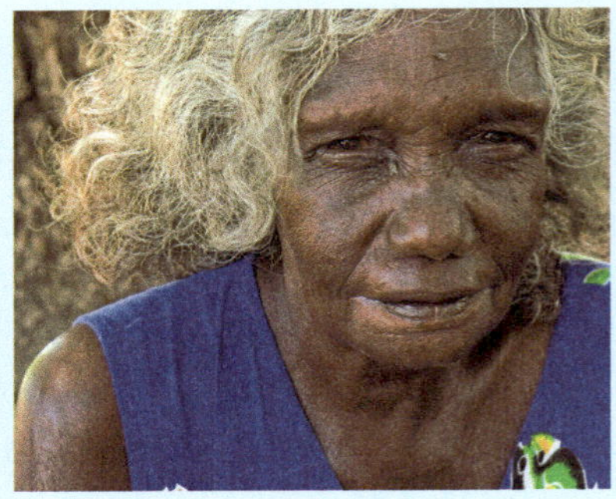

Australia is a country and also a continent with a huge desert at its centre. Most of its cities are near the coast, like the biggest cities, Sydney and Perth. The capital, Canberra, has lots of woods and farms around it. Australia is famous for its wildlife and its landscape. From Uluru in the centre to the Great Barrier Reef to Sydney, there is something for everyone. You can see lots of animals too, like kangaroos and koalas, and also thousands of types of fish, spiders and insects. There are lots of immigrants in Australia, but the Aboriginal people have been on the continent for over 50,000 years. Their traditions are very old. When British settlers arrived in the 18th century, they killed a lot of the Aboriginal people. Tourists from all around the world come to Australia for the 'sun, sea and surf' lifestyle.

Complete the facts about Australia.

Australia has big cities near the coast and a large (1) ______________ in the centre of the country. The capital, Canberra, has lots of (2) ______________ and (3) ______________ around it. Australia's wildlife and its (4) ______________ are famous attractions. You can also see lots of different animals like kangaroos, koalas, (5) ______________________________ (three examples). The Aboriginal people have lived in Australia for (6) ______________ 50,000 years. They have very old (7) ______________. A lot of the Aboriginals were killed when (8) ______________________ came to the country in the 18th century.

___/10P

Ziel 2: Ich kann einen Blogeintrag über eine Reise schreiben.

→p. 12/2

Fill in the gaps with the right form of the verbs in brackets.

Hi everyone,

I (1) ______________ (meet) Aboriginal people when I (2) ______________ (visit) Uluru last year. One of them (3) ______________ (talk) to me. He (4) ______________ (tell) us lots about the Aboriginal traditions. I (5) ___________ (be) sad, because we (6) ____________________ (not climb) Uluru. But we even (7) ______________ (eat) kangaroo meat. I (8) ______________ (be) surprised that I (9) ______________ (like) it. I (10) ________________ (write) more tomorrow.

Bye, Mona

Ziel 3: Ich kann darüber sprechen, wenn ich krank bin.

___ /4P

→p. 12/3

Finish the sentences.

1 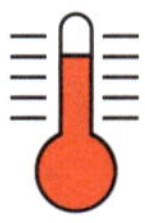
2 
3 
4 

1. I think I have a ______________________________
2. I feel hot and I have a ______________________________
3. If I don't feel better, I'll go ______________________________
4. If it helps, I'll take some ______________________________

Ziel 4: Ich kann Texte über Umweltprobleme verstehen.

___ /7P

→p. 13/4

Read the text on page 9 again. Tick ✓ right, wrong or not in the text.

	right	wrong	not in the text
1. The farmhouse was on fire.	☐	☐	☐
2. They put the sheep into the cages.	☐	☐	☐
3. Helicopters came and dropped water on the fires.	☐	☐	☐
4. The farm workers used the helicopters to leave the farm.	☐	☐	☐
5. One of the workers gave Sonya a little kangaroo.	☐	☐	☐
6. The baby kangaroo's mother ran away from the fire.	☐	☐	☐
7. Everybody stayed at the farm and watched the fire carefully.	☐	☐	☐

Ziel 5: Ich kann Informationen in einer Apotheke weitergeben.

___ /9P

→p. 13/5

When I came home from school today I felt really bad ☹. So I decided to go to a pharmacy. "I have a headache and I feel hot," I told the pharmacist. He answered, "I think you've caught a cold. It's best to take one tablet after breakfast and one before you go to bed for five days. You also need to drink lots of water." I was worried and said, "Now I can't take part in the talent show on Saturday. That means no singing for a few days!" The pharmacist told me, "Don't worry. You'll be OK. But if you aren't better by the end of the week, you'll have to see a doctor."

Lily Peterson, 15, aus Canberra in Australien hat dir diese Nachricht geschrieben. Gib die Aussagen sinngemäß auf Deutsch wieder.

Lily sagte dem Apotheker, dass sie ____________________ habe und ihr heiß sei. Der Apotheker vermutete, dass sie ____________________ habe. Er riet ihr, __________ Tage lang __________ ____________________ und eine vor dem Schlafengehen einzunehmen. Er sagte auch, sie müsse ____________________. Lily war ____________________ und erzählte ihm, dass sie dann am ______________________________ ____________________ und die nächsten Tage ______________________________.
Der Apotheker machte ihr Mut. Bis dahin gehe es ihr wieder gut. Sie müsse aber zum Arzt gehen, wenn es ______________________________.

Lösungen online z53m6b

○ Ziel 1: Ich kann Informationen über Australien verstehen.

About 30 million years ago, the Australian continent broke away from Antarctica.
There are some animals that only live in Australia, for example the koala and the kangaroo. Australia is famous for its coasts and landscape, but there are also a lot of big cities like Sydney and Perth. Australians like to spend a lot of time at the beach, where they have parties and do sport. In the centre of Australia, the outback, there are big farms. Only a few people live there. There are often no schools or hospitals near the farms. Children have their school lessons online.

Tick ✓ right, wrong or not in the text.

	right	wrong	not in the text
1. The Australian continent broke away from Africa.	☐	☐	☐
2. The koala and the kangaroo only live in Australia.	☐	☐	☐
3. A lot of famous Australians live on the coast.	☐	☐	☐
4. Australia is famous for its high mountains.	☐	☐	☐
5. Australian people love parties at the beach.	☐	☐	☐
6. Lots of people live in the outback.	☐	☐	☐
7. There are no schools for children in the outback.	☐	☐	☐
8. There is always a small hospital near a farm.	☐	☐	☐

○ Ziel 2: Ich kann einen Blogeintrag über eine Reise schreiben.

Read the text. Circle the right answer.

I (1) **go** • **went** to Australia last winter and I (2) **got** • **get** some great tips before I (3) **leave** • **left** Germany. Remember them for your next trip. I (4) **visit** • **visited** interesting places and (5) **spoke** • **speak** to some Aboriginal people. I (6) **didn't climb** • **climbed** Uluru because it is not allowed to do so. But I (7) **eat** • **ate** kangaroo meat and I (8) **liked** • **will like** it. Try it – you (9) **will be** • **were** surprised.

○ Ziel 3: Ich kann darüber sprechen, wenn ich krank bin.

Finish the sentences.

I'll make an appointment | I'll go to the pharmacy | I'll get | I'll have to stay

1. If I want to get better, ______________________ in bed.

2. If I need some medicine, ______________________.

3. If I don't feel better by next week, ______________________ at the doctor's.

4. If I go to the doctor's, ______________________ some good advice.

○ Ziel 4: Ich kann Texte über Umweltprobleme verstehen.

Read the text on page 9 again. Who did it? Write down the right names next to the statements.

Sonya and Rachel | Ally | workers

1. … woke up one night and shouted, “Fire!” ____________________
2. … told everybody what to do. ____________________
3. … moved the sheep into the fields. ____________________
4. … put the pets and the chickens into the cages. ____________________
5. … got things ready to leave the farm. ____________________
6. … found a baby kangaroo on the road. ____________________
7. … decided to stay on the farm. ____________________
8. … told one group to protect the house. ____________________
9. … were happy but still a little nervous. ____________________

○ Ziel 5: Ich kann Informationen in einer Apotheke weitergeben.

When I came home from school today I felt really bad ☹. I went to a pharmacy. I said to the pharmacist, “I have a bad headache.” He answered, “Take one of these tablets after breakfast and one before you go to bed for five days. Don’t forget to drink lots of water.” I told him, “I’m so sad because I can’t take part in the talent show on Saturday!” The pharmacist said, “If you aren’t better by Friday, you’ll have to see a doctor.”

Lily Peterson, 15, aus Canberra in Australien hat dir diese Nachricht geschrieben. Streiche die falschen Angaben durch.

1. Lily kam **heute** • **gestern** aus der Schule und fühlte sich richtig schlecht.
2. Deshalb ging sie **zum Arzt** • **zur Apotheke**.
3. Lily sagte dem Apotheker, dass sie fürchterliche **Kopfschmerzen** • **Halsschmerzen** habe.
4. Er riet ihr, eine Tablette **vor** • **nach** dem Frühstück und eine vor dem Schlafengehen zu nehmen.
5. Sie muss **die Tabletten fünf Tage lang nehmen** • **fünf Tage im Bett bleiben.**
6. Der Apotheker empfahl ihr außerdem, **kein** • **viel** Wasser zu trinken.
7. Das Schlimmste für Lily ist, **nicht an der Talentshow teilnehmen** • **nicht sprechen** zu können.
8. Wenn es ihr bis Freitag nicht besser geht, soll sie **zu einer anderen Apotheke** • **zum Arzt** gehen.

A picture-based interview

29/1 **1 Describe the picture.**

in front of | in the foreground | in the background | on the left | on the right
behind | in the middle | next to | on the right

Write down the first six words in the right place next to the picture. Then complete the sentences with all the words.

This picture shows a landscape with people and wildlife. ____________ you can see two people. They are ____________ of the picture. The young woman is ____________, the young man is ____________ her. There are two groups of kangaroos ____________ them. We can see two kangaroos ____________ and two kangaroos ____________. ____________ there are some mountains. They are ____________ a lake.

29/2 **2 Answer the interview questions about the picture.**

wear | stand | watch | eat | be hungry | not rain | be cloudy | be happy

What are the people wearing?	The young man *is wearing* ____________
	The young woman *is* ____________
What are the people doing?	They *are* ____________
	and they ____________
What are the kangaroos doing?	They ____________ because they ____________
What's the weather like?	The weather is OK. It ____________ but ____________
How do the people feel?	I think they ____________ because they can watch the animals.

Ein zweisprachiges Wörterbuch in Printform ist für die gesamte schriftliche Prüfung erlaubt.

Hör-Dateien online
wz68ud

A Listening Comprehension (Hörverstehen)

4 **1 Listen to an Australian teenager talking about her life. There is one mistake in each sentence. Cross out the wrong words and correct them. There is an example (0.) at the beginning.**

0. Laura lives with her parents and ~~grandparents~~ in the outback. sister
1. Their farm is in Queensland near a small mountain. ______
2. There are no kids. ______
3. The weather is really wet at the moment. ______
4. The family has to check if the cows have enough food and trees that can protect them from the sun. ______
5. The teachers often meet for a barbecue. ______
6. A doctor comes once a month. ______
7. Laura would like to be a doctor one day. ______

5 **2 Listen to Simon from Sydney. Answer the questions. Write short answers. There is an example (0.) at the beginning.**

0. How does Simon get to school? — By bike.
1. Does he enjoy going to school? — No, he doesn't. He finds it ______.
2. What is Simon's favourite thing to do? — ______ and ______.
3. Who says that he has to work harder at school? — ______
4. What does Simon do with his friends at the weekend? — He goes to the ______, does some ______ or has a ______ or a pool party.
5. Why is Bondi Beach the best place? — You can go ______ and ______ there.
6. Why do people put up flags at Bondi Beach? — They show you where you are ______.
7. What does Simon want to be one day? — A ______ at Bondi Beach.

B Use of English (Sprachgebrauch)

1 Australia

Write the word that matches the definition. There is an example (0.) at the beginning.

0. A dangerous Australian creature in the water c r o c o d i l e
1. An area in Australia far away from towns _ _ _ _ _ _ _
2. The red rock in the centre of Australia _ _ _ _ _
3. People from Australia with old traditions _ _ _ _ _ _ _ _ _ _ _ _ _ _ _ _
4. The capital of Australia _ _ _ _ _ _ _ _
5. Two animals which only live in Australia _ _ _ _ _ and _ _ _ _ _ _ _ _
6. The biggest city in Australia _ _ _ _ _ _
7. Australian people often come together for it _ _ _ _ _ _ _ _
8. Perfect waves are good for this kind of sport _ _ _ _ _ _ _

2 Travelling

Complete the text using the correct words from the box. There are extra words in the box. There is an example (0) at the beginning.

about • at • between • for • from • in • in • near • of • on • ~~to~~ • to • under • up • with

Good morning, everyone.

Welcome (0) *to* ________ our short flight to Perth this morning.

The flight takes (1) ________ 30 minutes.

We will arrive in Perth (2) ________ about 7:30.

Please stay (3) ________ your seats during the flight.

The bags and suitcases are now (4) ________ the plane.

The pilot is making his last checks (5) ________ the flight.

We will be (6) ________ the air in ten minutes.

There is a bottle (7) ________ water for each of you. Please help yourself.

The weather today is fine. It is warm and dry (8) ________ some clouds in the sky.

You will have a nice view (9) ________ the air.

I hope you'll enjoy our flight (10) ________ Perth this morning.

3 At Ally's farm

Ally is talking to some new workers at her farm.
Fill in the right form of the verb. There is an example (0) at the beginning.

G'day. My name (0) _is_ ______ (be) Ally and I'm going to show you our farm. I (1) ______________ (can give) you all the information you need. This (2) ______________ (be) your home for the next three months and we all want you to be happy here. The work on our farm (3) ______________ (not be) easy. Each of you will have to do jobs every day. Our day always (4) ______________ (start) at 6:30 a.m. We usually (5) ______________ (have) a little snack together. Then we have to feed the horses and the sheep. At 8:30 a.m. everyone (6) ______________ (have) breakfast. After breakfast we always check the animals which (7) ______________ (not be) on the farm. You can all drive and there (8) ______________ (be) three tractors that you can use. We (9) ______________ (not meet) for lunch. In the evening we always (10) ______________ (eat) together and (11) ______________ (talk) about the good things and the problems. By 10:00 p.m. you will be in bed. (12) ______________ you ______________ (have) any questions?

4 Tourist questions about Uluru

Read the questions and find a matching answer on the right. You don't need all of the answers. There is an example (0.) at the beginning.

Tourist

0. How old is Uluru?
1. Can we go up to the top of Uluru today?
2. Why can't we climb Uluru?
3. What can you do at Uluru?
4. Is there a guide for us?
5. Is there anything more exciting to do?
6. What about Aboriginal traditions?

Guide

a) Because Aboriginals today have a modern lifestyle.
b) The Aboriginals have a lot of traditions like special dances and playing the didgeridoo.
c) Yes, a guide shows you the way and some interesting dot paintings.
d) You can walk around the rock.
e) Of course, you can go on a helicopter flight around the rock.
f) It is about 550 million years old.
g) Because it is an important place for the Aboriginal people.
h) They have lived here for over 50,000 years.
i) No, sorry. You aren't allowed to climb Uluru.

0	1	2	3	4	5	6
f						

C Reading Comprehension (Leseverstehen)

The Royal Flying Doctor Service (RFDS)[1]

A What happens when you live in the outback and you are seriously ill? Or you need some medicine? Well, you call the Royal Flying Doctor Service.

B John Flynn wanted to help people who lived far away from medical help. In 1928 he started his experiment and it has now become a service that has about 70 planes. They fly over 20 million kilometres every year and help people in an area of 7.7 million square kilometres. The service can fly to any place in the country, even if it is very far away.

C The Royal Flying Doctor Service became famous around the world in the 1980s with a TV series which was called *The Flying Doctors*. However, Mia Jefferies, who has worked as a 'flying doctor' for over ten years, explains that the doctors' job is not always as exciting as shown on TV. "Most people imagine that the flying doctors save people after a dangerous animal attack or because they have fallen down a mountain," she says. "But most of the time the doctors work in small hospitals in one of the towns in the outback. We deal with normal, everyday problems, do check-ups and give out medicine. Of course, some people have more serious problems and we fly patients to bigger hospitals. And if a person is seriously ill, we fly out to them. But often we can give people medical advice on the phone, and most farms have medicine available which they can use then."

D The RFDS not only saves lives, it also had another great idea: in 1944 John Flynn's teacher and friend Adelaide Miethke travelled to children in the outback and listened to their problems. She then thought about using the Royal Flying Doctor Service radio network for children. In 1951 there was the first lesson by today's School of the Air for children in the outback.

1 The Royal Flying Doctor Service (RFDS) – *fliegender Ärztedienst in Australien*

1 Which paragraph is it? Write the correct letter (A–D). There is an example (0.) at the beginning.

Which paragraph tells you …

0. … that the doctors can often help on the phone? C
1. … who you can call in the outback when you are seriously ill? ☐
2. … about the year of the first School of the Air lesson? ☐
3. … that the doctors' job is not as exciting as shown on TV? ☐
4. … the number of kilometres the doctors fly every year? ☐

2 Answer the questions. There is an example (0.) at the beginning.

0. When did John Flynn start his service to help ill people in the outback? In 1928.
1. What do a lot of people think about the flying doctors' job? (2 facts) ____________________

____
2. Where do the doctors work most of the time? ____________________
3. What does a flying doctor do with people who have serious problems? (2 facts) ____________________

____

D Text Production (Schreiben)

1 **Du schreibst eine persönliche E-Mail an deine Gastfamilie in Australien.**

Du hast die Möglichkeit, acht Wochen als Austausch-Schüler/in in Australien zu verbringen. Schreibe eine E-Mail an deine Gastfamilie.

- Bedanke dich und stelle dich vor (Name, Alter).
- Erzähle von deiner Schule und sage, was du daran magst (z.B. Lieblingsfächer) und was nicht.
- Sage, was du gerne in deiner Freizeit machst und für was du dich interessierst (z.B. Hobbies, Sport, Musik).
- Erzähle auch von deinen Haustieren oder was du gerne isst.
- Stelle 1-2 Fragen, z.B. zu Haustieren, dem Zuhause oder den Hobbies deiner Gastfamilie.
- Stelle eine weitere Frage zu der Schule, auf die du in Australien gehen wirst, oder zu Freizeitmöglichkeiten in der Nähe.
- Sage, warum du gerne nach Australien reisen möchtest.

Schreibe eine E-Mail von ungefähr 100 Wörtern. Achte auf eine ansprechende äußere Form und eine gut lesbare Handschrift.

E-MAIL

Dear Mr and Mrs Wilson,

Thank you very much for the invitation to stay with your family in ...

E Mediation (Sprachmittlung)

Dein Freund Toni ist ein echter Australien-Fan. In diesem Jahr wird er mit seinen Eltern und seiner achtjährigen Schwester, die im Rollstuhl sitzt, über Weihnachten in Australien sein. In Sydney möchten sie dann gerne eine Touristenattraktion besuchen. Im Internet findet dein Freund folgende Angebote und bittet dich um Hilfe.

INTERNET

Whale watching tours from Sydney

$68.00 per person (online price) • 2 hrs 45 mins • from June to November

- tours in English, French and German
- boat with large windows and large open-air decks
- see great sights of Sydney on your way
- see whales on their journey to the Great Barrier Reef
- wheelchair accessible
- starting point is near public transport
- not for children under 3

Blue Mountains Day Trip

$200.00 per person (online price) • 10 hrs • max. number of people: 20

- tours in English
- visit to Sydney Zoo: see kangaroos, wombats and koalas
- visit to Blue Mountains National Park: ride the world's steepest railway and cable car, walk high up in the rainforest
- go shopping for souvenirs in a pretty village
- free lunch and dinner
- boat tour back to Sydney
- free shuttle service to your hotel
- not for children under 8

Sydney Pass

$59.00 per person (online price) • valid for 1 month

- you can choose three out of 30 sights or tours
- includes Sydney Sea Aquarium, Sydney Tower Eye, the zoo and many boat or bus tours
- no queues as your pass lets you go directly to the entrance
- all sights are wheelchair accessible and near public transport
- no shuttle service to your hotel

Hop-on hop-off bus tour of Sydney

$45.00 per person (online price or pay at the bus entrance) • 2 hrs • double-decker bus

- tours in English, French, German, Italian, Spanish, Turkish and Chinese
- tickets valid for 24 hours
- audio guide with information about sights and history of city
- hop off the bus and look at your favourite sight then hop on the next bus that comes along
- free internet
- wheelchair accessible (not on top deck)

1 **Lies die Texte zu den vier Ausflugsmöglichkeiten in Sydney. Vergleiche sie. Schreibe zu jeder Attraktion stichpunktartig nützliche Informationen auf Deutsch auf. Beantworte zuletzt die Frage unten auf Deutsch.**

Whale watching	Vorteile:	______
	Kosten:	______
	Nachteile:	______

Sydney Pass	Vorteile:	______ ______
	Kosten:	______
	Nachteile:	______

Blue Mountains	Vorteile:	______
	Kosten:	______
	Nachteile:	______

Hop-on hop-off bus tour	Vorteile:	______ ______
	Kosten:	______
	Nachteile:	______

Welche Attraktion empfiehlst du Tonis Familie?
Was ist a) kostengünstig? b) am interessantesten? c) am besten für alle in der Familie geeignet?
Begründe deine Entscheidung.

______

______

______

______

______

______

______

______

______

Hör-Dateien online
wz68ud

Exploring India

36/2
1 A quiz about India

a) What do you know about India? Test yourself.

1. India is …
   - ☐ as big as Germany.
   - ☐ not as big as Germany.
   - ☐ a lot bigger than Germany.

2. More than … people live in India.
   - ☐ 1,000,000,000 people
   - ☐ 10,000,000,000 people
   - ☐ 100,000,000,000 people

3. A lot of poor people live in …
   - ☐ colonies.
   - ☐ the Taj Mahal.
   - ☐ slums.

4. There are … official languages in India.
   - ☐ two
   - ☐ 22
   - ☐ millions of

5. Most people in India work …
   - ☐ in Europe.
   - ☐ in slums.
   - ☐ on farms.

6. Until 1947 India was a …
   - ☐ British company.
   - ☐ British colony.
   - ☐ British problem.

7. Mahatma Gandhi fought for …
   - ☐ India's independence.
   - ☐ the computer industry.
   - ☐ more official languages.

8. International companies are interested in Indian people because they can speak …
   - ☐ Chinese.
   - ☐ German.
   - ☐ English.

9. But the country has a lot of … problems too, for example with waste.
   - ☐ environmental
   - ☐ traditional
   - ☐ computer

10. … and traditions are very important in India.
    - ☐ Pollution
    - ☐ Family
    - ☐ Protests

b) Check your answers. You get 1 point for every right answer.

10 points	Wow! That's great! You are an expert.
7–9 points	Well done! You already know a lot about India.
4–6 points	You did OK.
0–3 points	Read the texts about India again and find the right answers.

38/2 1 Find the words for the crossword.

1. The leader of a company is the …
2. The Taj Mahal is a famous building in …
3. A city in the north of India.
4. All the things in a shop are …
5. This thing helps to produce car parts.
6. IT stands for information …
7. The place where you work on a computer, for example, is an …
8. Another word for right is …
9. A person who buys things is a …
10. A city in the south of India.

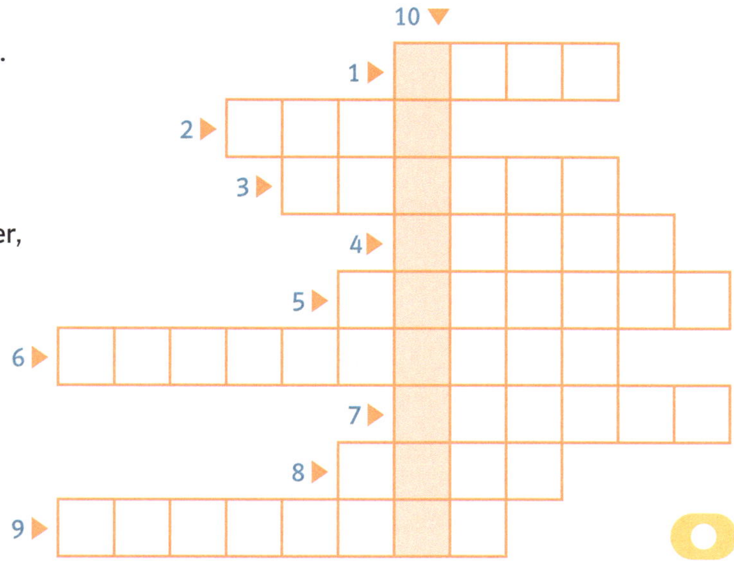

39/5 2 Find a job for each sentence. You don't need all the jobs.

tour guide · farmer · chef · computer programmer · police officer · receptionist · nurse · factory worker · doctor · travel agent

1. A ______________________ works in a hotel, for example, and answers the guests' questions.
2. A ______________________ shows tourists around and tells them about the history of sights.
3. A ______________________ helps you to find and book your holiday.
4. A ______________________ designs new software.
5. A ______________________ often works on an assembly line of a company.
6. A ______________________ cooks food in restaurants and hotels.

6 39/6 3 (LISTENING) Listen to Sarah and Tom talking about their trip to Jaipur. Circle the right word.

1. Jaipur's **old** • **new** city is also called the Pink City.
2. In 1876 people in Jaipur painted the walls pink for the **Prince of Jaipur** • **Prince of Wales**.
3. Sarah wants to go on a **hip hop tour** • **hop-on hop-off tour**.
4. Tom would love to go on a **hot** • **high** air balloon ride.
5. But the balloon ride is too **far away** • **expensive** for them.
6. They then visited the Palace of Winds with its **953** • **593** little windows.

40/8

4 (WRITING) Make sentences.

a) Use the simple present.

1. I always ____________ (get up) at 6 o'clock in the morning.
2. My sister never ____________ (have) breakfast at home.
3. My parents ____________ (go) to work by bus every day.
4. My friend Lasse and I often ____________ (meet) at the weekend.
5. Lasse ____________ (not have) any brothers or sisters.
6. We usually ____________ (go) shopping at the market on Saturdays.
7. Mum sometimes ____________ (make) a pizza for us on Saturday evenings.
8. My friends and I ____________ (not go) to the cinema very often. It's too expensive.

He, she, it, das ‚s' muss mit!

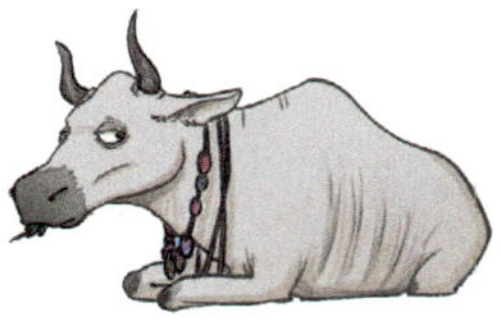

b) Write four more sentences about you, your friends or your family.

9. ____________
10. ____________
11. ____________
12. ____________

5 (WRITING) What do you and your friends do at the weekend?

40/8

Use the signal words. You can use the ideas in the box or your own ideas.

> get up late • go shopping • meet friends ✓ • go to the cinema • play football • go running • play with the dog • bake a cake • make pizza • do homework • clean … • meet in town • hang out at • spend much time online / on social media

1. (always) *I always meet my friends on Saturday afternoon.*
2. (always) ____________
3. (never) ____________
4. (sometimes) ____________
5. (often) ____________
6. (usually) ____________
7. (never) ____________
8. (often) ____________

40/8

6 What are you good at? What do you like? What don't you like? Complete the sentences. Use a verb + -ing. Here are some ideas.

write texts | listen to people | talk about films | prepare and cook food | tidy my room | work on the computer | communicate on the phone | work with a partner | discuss topics | do sports | play computer games | go on holiday | watch the news | speak English

1. I'm good at communicating on the phone.
2. I'm good at ______
3. I enjoy ______
4. I don't like ______
5. I hate ______
6. I can't stand ______
7. I look forward to ______
8. I like ______

41/10

7 (SPEAKING) An interview with Kashida

Kashida meets an old school friend. Make a dialogue and act it with a partner.

Kashida's friend	Kashida
Du freust dich, Kashida zu treffen und fragst, ob ihr der neue Job als Reiseleiterin gefällt. Hi, good to see you, Kashida. Do you ______	Begrüße deine/n Freund/in und antworte, dass dir dein neuer Job sehr gefällt. Hi, good to see you too. ______
Frage, um wie viel Uhr sie mit der Arbeit beginnt. What time ______	Antworte, dass du normalerweise um 10 Uhr anfängst. ______
Frage, wie viele Stunden sie am Tag arbeitet. ______	Sage, dass du jeden Tag vier Stunden arbeitest. ______
Frage, wie groß die Touristengruppen sind. ______	Antworte, zwischen 5 und 20 Personen. ______
Sage, dass sich das alles toll anhört. Frage, ob du morgen mitkommen kannst. ______	Sage ja, natürlich. Freue dich, dass er/sie mitkommen möchte. ______

42/1

1 Read the text on page 42 in your book again.

a) Put the sentences in the correct order.

- [ ] Drinking water is not available everywhere. People have to walk long distances for it.
- [ ] Today farmers change their crops or people raise money for better sanitation and drinking water.
- [ ] A lot of people don't have toilets or bathrooms. They use the rivers to wash everything.
- [ ] Teenagers in India worry about different environmental problems in their country.
- [ ] Fertilisers and the fact that the farmers grow two or three different crops in the same field every year damage the soil.

b) Write the sentences from a) in the correct order in your exercise book and you'll get a short summary of the article.

43/5

2 (SOUNDS) Listen, read and say.

a) Match the English phrases with their German meaning.

1. environmental problems	b) Dünger benutzen
2. sustainable farming	s) sanitäre Anlagen
3. waste and pollution	m) Geld sammeln
4. use fertilisers	e) verschiedene Feldfrüchte anbauen
5. damage the soil	p) Umweltprobleme
6. grow different crops	o) Abfall und Verschmutzung
7. raise money	l) dem Boden schaden
8. sanitation	r) nachhaltige Landwirtschaft

In the correct order, the letters on the right make a new word:

____

7 b) Listen and say the English sentences.

1. There‿are‿a‿lot‿of‿environmental‿problems‿in‿India.
2. People‿need‿to‿make‿farming‿more‿sustainable.
3. There‿is‿a‿lot‿of‿waste‿and‿pollution.
4. Farmers‿use‿fertilisers which‿are‿slowly‿damaging‿the‿soil.
5. They‿grow‿different‿crops‿in‿the‿same‿field.
6. Some‿villages‿have‿raised‿money‿for‿better‿sanitation.

7 c) Listen and circle ◯ the stressed syllable.

1. p r o b l e m s	4. f e r t i l i s e r s
2. s u s t a i n a b l e	5. d a m a g i n g
3. p o l l u t i o n	6. s a n i t a t i o n

44/6 ↗ **3** **Put the words in the correct boxes.**

in the big cities · well · every year · here · to the next village · in the future · fast · in rivers · slowly · in the same field · carefully · for many years · yesterday · very hard · tomorrow

Adverbien des Ortes Wo? Wohin? Woher? **Place – Where?**	Adverbien der Zeit Wann? Wie lange? Seit wann? **Time – When?**	Adverbien der Art und Weise Wie macht jemand etwas? **How?**

44/7 ↗ **4** **Write sentences about life in India.**

Use the pictures and words below and write two correct sentences for each picture.

Remember!
Place before time!
Ort vor Zeit!

1. at the Taj Mahal • Kashida • every week • shows tourists around
2. She • very well • different languages • speaks

3. all day • cows • You can see • in many places around India
4. They slowly • in the crowded streets • every day • walk around

5. from another village • water • every day • have to get • Some people
6. use • A lot of Indian people • very carefully • drinking water

45/8

5 Read Deepali's blog on page 45 in your book again and answer the questions.

1. Is village life in India the same as in Europe?
   - ☐ No, it's different.
   - ☐ No, it's not difficult.
   - ☐ Yes, it is.
2. Why do most Indian people have eggs at home? Because a lot of them have …
   - ☐ neighbours with chickens.
   - ☐ chickens themselves.
   - ☐ fried chickens.
3. What do Indian people like to do with their neighbours?
   - ☐ Work on a chicken farm.
   - ☐ Sell chickens at the market.
   - ☐ Chat with each other.
4. Where do lots of Indian people get their drinking water from?
   - ☐ From their house.
   - ☐ From their neighbour's house.
   - ☐ From another village.
5. How do lots of Indian people get to other villages?
   - ☐ They just walk.
   - ☐ They go by bus.
   - ☐ They go by boat.
6. What does Deepali want to know from you?
   - ☐ Nice things and places in your hometown.
   - ☐ The number of teenagers in your hometown.
   - ☐ Where you live.

45/9

6 Complete the text with the words from the box. You don't need all the words.

a • at • beautiful • cows • day • drink • for
grow • in • Indian • living • ~~national~~
that • there • to • who

India has a lot of interesting (1) *national* ____________ parks.

All in all there are about (2) ____________ hundred of them.

You can see so many different wild animals in (3) ____________ landscapes.

There are high mountains and (4) ____________ is also the coast and the beaches.

If you want (5) ____________ see a tiger, go (6) ____________ April or May.

That is the Indian summer and the wild cats go to the water holes to (7) ____________.

Tigers sleep (8) ____________ night. So if you want to see one, go during the (9) ____________.

But it is not only tigers (10) ____________ you can see in India. There are also bears and wolves,

(11) ____________ example. And don't forget the (12) ____________ in the streets.

45/10

7 (SPEAKING) Prepare a one-minute talk.

facts about India • farming in India
environmental problems in India

Du findest Informationen zu jedem Thema in der Unit. Sammle, wähle aus und trage vor.

Choose one of the topics. Take notes (five or more). Then talk about your topic.

48/1 1 (MEDIATION) Jobs in India

1 My name is Krishna. I'm 19 years old. I live in Varanasi and work as a tour guide here. Varanasi is one of the oldest cities in India. It is situated along the river Ganges and it is the 'Holy City' for Hindus and Buddhists. Many tourists visit it because it is a city of temples, religion, tradition and culture. During the week I go to university and study Indian history. At the weekends I earn some extra money as a guide. I meet a lot of people from all over the world in my job. That's why all guides have to speak at least three different languages. The tourists like the temples and the 'ghats'. These are places along the river Ganges which are used for bathing and religious ceremonies.

2 I'm Noor and I'm a computer programmer. I finished my education at programming college seven months ago. Then I started to work for a small IT company in New Delhi. I work with 11 other people in a large office and we all write computer programs. My job never gets boring because we work for a number of different customers in India, Europe and Japan. Sometimes it isn't easy to solve difficult IT problems quickly. However, the best thing is that we can help each other. We really have to work hard every day and most of us earn less money than the programmers in Europe.

a) Lies Text 1 und ergänze die Informationen auf Deutsch.

Krishna studiert ____________________ in Varanasi. Varanasi ist eine der ältesten Städte Indiens und liegt am ____________________. Für ____________________ ist Varanasi die ‚Heilige Stadt'. Krishna arbeitet an den Wochenenden als ____________________, um sich extra Geld zu verdienen. Er trifft ____________________. Deshalb muss man in seinem Job mindestens ____________________. Die Touristen lieben ____________________ und die Ghats entlang des Ganges in Varanasi. Ghats sind Böschungen, an denen Menschen sich reinigen und ____________________ Zeremonien abhalten.

● b) Fasse den Inhalt von Text 2 auf Deutsch zusammen.
Orientiere dich an folgenden Schlüsselwörtern.

Beruf • Ausbildung • Arbeitsbedingungen • Kunden • Probleme • Verdienst

Noor ist eine ____________________

____

____

____

____

____

____

46/3 1 Facts about Gandhi's life

Read the article on pages 46 and 47 in your book again. Write down the right words in each sentence.

1. Gandhi's first name was M o h a n d a s.
2. Gandhi wanted India to become an _ _ _ _ ☐ _ _ _ _ _ _ country.
3. Gandhi showed the Indian people how to _ _ _ ☐ their own salt.
4. A lot of Indians followed Gandhi and protested without using _ _ ☐ _ _ _ _ _ _.
5. However, there was violence between Hindus and _ _ _ _ _ _ ☐.
6. Gandhi himself was a Hindu and he _ _ _ _ _ _ ☐ _ _ other religions.
7. When he was friendly to Muslims in India, some people became _ _ _ ☐ _.
8. In 1948 Gandhi was killed by a Hindu _ _ _ _ _ _ _ _ _ ☐.

Put the letters from the boxes in a) in the right order and complete the sentence:

The Salt March was a peaceful ☐☐☐☐☐☐☐ against the British.

46/3 2 Complete the text about Mahatma Gandhi.

Choose the correct words from the box. You don't need all the words.

arranged • at • became • colony ✓ • didn't wear • for • law • lawyer • many • much • of • peaceful • soul • to • up • vegetarian • wore

When India was a British (1) colony ________, many Indians were very poor and had to work very hard. Mahatma Gandhi wanted (2) ____________ change the lives of the poorest in India. He fought (3) ____________ his country's independence. Gandhi's fight was (4) ________________ because he believed in non-violent protests. He (5) ____________ simple clothes and didn't eat meat because he was a (6) ________________. He looked small but he was strong and he didn't give (7) ____________. He broke the (8) ____________ when he told the Indian people how to make their own salt. Gandhi went to prison (9) ____________ times. Indian people called Gandhi 'Mahatma', which means 'great (10) ____________'.

47/4

3 (READING) Read the text about a famous Indian woman.

Indira Gandhi (1917–1984)

A Indira Gandhi was the first woman to become prime minister[1] of India. She was prime minister from 1966 to 1977 and from 1980 to 1984. Indira Gandhi was born as Indira Nehru on 19th November 1917. She was the only child of Jawaharlal and Kamala Nehru. As a child Indira often spent time alone because her father was away a lot (sometimes, like Mahatma Gandhi, even in prison) and her mother was very ill. Kamala died in 1936. Indira went to different schools and universities in India and Europe. At university in England, she met her future husband Feroze Gandhi. They went back to India, got married in 1942 and had two sons, Rajiv and Sanjay.

B When India became independent in 1947, Indira's father became the country's first prime minister. Indira became his assistant. She soon started her own career and became prime minister in 1966. It was not easy for Indira as a woman. A lot of people in India did not have jobs or enough food.

C In the 1970s, however, India turned from a country that needed help into a country that grew great crops. More farmland, the use of fertilisers, different water systems and modern technology made farming successful in India. The country could finally feed itself.

D However, some people hated Indira for what she did. She had put many people in prison. In 1977 she didn't become prime minister again. But three years later she did. Again the situation was not easy. The Sikhs, a religious group, fought for their independence and there was a lot of violence. In 1984 Indira Gandhi sent in soldiers against them and many Sikhs were killed. On 31st October 1984 Indira Gandhi was shot by her own Sikh bodyguards. Her son Rajiv Gandhi became the next prime minister.

1 prime minister – *Premierminister/in*

47/4

4 Which paragraph tells you ...

1. ... how India managed to grow enough food? ☐
2. ... why it was difficult for Indira to be prime minister? ☐
3. ... about Indira's education and family? ☐
4. ... why some people did not like Indira? ☐

47/4

5 Answer the questions. Write short answers.

1. What was special about Indira Gandhi? ______
2. What do you know about her education? ______
3. When did India become independent? ______
4. Why did farming become successful in India in the 1970s? ______
______
5. What did some people hate Indira for? ______
6. Who killed Indira Gandhi in 1984? ______

Lösungen online f7ri5v

___ /6P Ziel 1: Ich kann Informationen über Indien verstehen.

→p. 34/1

India is famous for its food, films, culture, wildlife and history.

A lot of tourists visit the country every year. It is the seventh largest country in the world with more than 1.3 billion people.

People in India speak many different languages and have different religions. Family and traditions are most important for Indian people. India's economy is growing fast and there are a lot of rich people in the country. However, there is a big difference between the lives of the rich and the poor people there. A lot of poor people move from villages to the bigger cities, where they hope to find better jobs. Many of them can't find good jobs. They don't earn enough money so they have to live in poor conditions in slums. The slums are usually dirty and there's a lot of rubbish in the streets. Big families often live in one small room. They don't have toilets, bathrooms or even clean water. A lot of people who live in the slums work in the city in the houses of richer people or they have jobs as factory workers. Children of these poor families often don't go to school because they have to earn money for their families. Organizations and the government are trying to improve the conditions in the slums. They raise money for better sanitation.

Answer the questions. Write short answers.

1. Which two facts say that India is very big? ______________________
2. Which two things are important for Indian people? ______________________
3. Why do so many people leave their villages? ______________________
4. Why do people live in slums? ______________________
5. What is the children's situation in the slums? ______________________

   ____
6. What does the government do to make the slums better? ______________________

___ /5P Ziel 2: Ich kann eine Firma vorstellen.

→p. 34/2

Look at the notes. Present the company you work for in an e-mail to a friend. Write down five facts.

Hi Max,

Let me present you the company I work for:

Sustainable Farming IT

____

____

____

____

____

I'll tell you more next time.

Bye, Sammy

Sustainable Farming IT
IT company in New Delhi
Job: write and sell computer programs for managing farms
Customers: farmers, no visits, work online
Workplace: large office
Team: 8 people, good conditions for working together

___ /6P

Ziel 3: Ich kann ein Poster über Nachhaltigkeit gestalten.

→p. 35/3

Complete the poster with the correct words from the box. You don't need all the words.

any • as • clothes • environment • environmental • grew • grow • public • some • vegetables

What WE can do for our ____________________:

Buy milk, eggs, fruit and ____________________ from farms in Bavaria.

Use ________________ transport to school from Monday to Friday.

Don't buy plastic bags ________________ more at the supermarket.

Raise money for ____________________ projects.

Let's ________________ potatoes and tomatoes in our gardens.

___ /6P

Ziel 4: Ich kann einen Text über eine berühmte Person verstehen.

→p. 35/4

Read the text on page 31 again. Answer the questions. Write short answers.

1. When was Indira Gandhi prime minister? ____________________
2. What happened in 1936? ____________________
3. Who became India's first prime minister in 1947? ____________________
4. What problems did India have in 1966? ____________________
5. What happened when India grew better crops in the 1970s? ____________________
6. What did the Sikhs fight for? ____________________

___ /4P

Ziel 5: Ich kann Informationen über verschiedene Jobs weitergeben.

→p. 35/5

Sita Kapoor, 19, has worked in her father's restaurant in Mumbai, India, since her 15th birthday. Every day she has to cut up meat and wash and cut vegetables. Sometimes she helps her dad to plan what they need to buy at the market. "Our food always has to taste and look good," she says. Sita works every evening from 5:00 p.m. until 10:00 p.m. "Occasionally I also have to work on Sundays. I like my job. One day I want to have my own restaurant."

Deine kleine Schwester sieht im Internet einen Bericht über eine junge indische Frau, die in einem Restaurant arbeitet. Sie versteht nicht alles, bittet dich um Hilfe und stellt dir eine paar Fragen. Beantworte die Fragen kurz auf Deutsch.

1. Hat Sita den Job im Restaurant zum 15. Geburtstag geschenkt bekommen? ____________________

   ____
2. Was tut sie dort außer Fleisch und Gemüse zuzubereiten? ____________________
3. Sie findet, dass das Essen immer gut aussehen muss. Was muss es noch? ____________________

Lösungen online f7ri5v

○ Ziel 1: Ich kann Informationen über Indien verstehen.

India is famous for its food, films, culture, wildlife and history. A lot of tourists visit the country every year. It is the seventh largest country in the world and over 1.3 billion people live there. People in India speak many different languages and have different religions. Family and traditions are very important in India. The economy is growing fast and there are a lot of rich people in the country. But there is a big difference between the lives of the rich and the poor people. A lot of poor people move from villages to the bigger cities because they want a better job. But it's hard to find a good job, so they have to live in slums. The slums are usually dirty and there's a lot of rubbish. Big families often live in one small room. They don't have toilets, bathrooms or clean water. Many of them work in the city in the houses of richer people or they have jobs as factory workers. Their children often don't go to school because they have to earn money for their families. Organizations and the government are trying to improve the conditions in the slums. They try to raise money for better sanitation and more flats.

Tick ✓ the right answers.

1. Many tourists visit India because of its …
   a) economy and religions. ☐
   b) culture and wildlife. ☐
2. Most people in India are interested in …
   a) different languages. ☐
   b) family and traditions. ☐
3. There's a big difference between …
   a) rich and poor people. ☐
   b) children in the slums and their parents. ☐
4. Many children in slums don't go to school because …
   a) schools are too far away. ☐
   b) they have to work to get money. ☐

○ Ziel 2: Ich kann eine Firma vorstellen.

Match the parts of the sentences.

1. Our IT company writes
2. The customers are
3. We usually don't meet
4. The IT office is
5. I work in
6. I like that because

a) our customers because we work online.
b) very big.
c) and sells computer programs.
d) a team of eight people.
e) we can work together easily.
f) farmers who need help to manage their farms.

○ Ziel 3: Ich kann ein Poster über Nachhaltigkeit gestalten.

Complete the poster with the correct words. Cross out the wrong words.

What WE can do for our **environment** • **sanitation**:

Buy milk, eggs, fruit and **vets** • **vegetables** from farms in Bavaria.

Use **public** • **pupil's** transport every day.

Don't buy **plastic bags** • **waste** any more at the supermarket.

Raise money **for** • **in** environmental projects.

Let's grow potatoes and tomatoes in our **houses** • **gardens.**

○ Ziel 4: Ich kann einen Text über eine berühmte Person verstehen.

Read the text on page 31 again. Complete the sentences with the right words from the box. You don't need all the words.

became • Europe • friends • husband • independent • Nehru • problems • put in prison • sons

1. Indira Gandhi was born as Indira ____________________, the only child of Jawaharlal and Kamala.
2. Indira was educated in India and in ____________________.
3. She met her later ____________________ Feroze Gandhi at university in England.
4. They had two ____________________, Rajiv and Sanjay.
5. Indira's father became prime minister when India became ____________________ in 1947.
6. Indira was killed in 1984. After that her son Rajiv ____________________ prime minister.

○ Ziel 5: Ich kann Informationen über verschiedene Jobs weitergeben.

Sita Kapoor, 19, has worked in her father's restaurant in Mumbai, India, since her 15th birthday. Every day she has to cut up meat and wash and cut vegetables. Sometimes she helps her dad to plan what they need to buy at the market. "Our food always has to taste and look good," she says. Sita works every evening from 5:00 p.m. until 10:00 p.m. "Occasionally I also have to work on Sundays. I like my job. One day I want to have my own restaurant."

Lies den Text und vervollständige die Sätze.

1. Sita Kapoor arbeitet seit ____________________ im Restaurant ihres Vaters in Mumbai.
2. Ihr Job ist es, Fleisch und ____________________ zuzubereiten.
3. Manchmal unterstützt sie ihren Vater auch bei der ____________________ für den Einkauf auf dem Markt.
4. Sie arbeitet täglich ____________________ am Abend, manchmal auch ____________________.
5. Sita träumt davon, später einmal ein ____________________ zu haben.

A picture-based story

Amy and Derek are from London. Last year their parents had a fantastic present for them, a trip to …

A. New Delhi, last year in June

B. The next day

C. At the Taj Mahal in Agra

55/1 **1 Look at the pictures and the texts. Take notes.**

What? present, ____________________

____

Who? ____________________

____

Where? ____________________

____

When? ____________________

____

55/2 **2 Put in the correct simple past form.**

It (1) ____________ (be) a long flight. Amy and Derek finally (2) ____________ (arrive) at New Delhi Airport. They (3) ____________ (decide) to take a taxi to their hotel. Suddenly the taxi driver (4) ____________ (stop).

"Why (5) ____________ you ____________ (stop)?" Amy (6) ____________ (ask).

"We must wait. Cows are sacred in India," the driver (7) ____________ (answer).

55/2 **3** **Use adjectives or adverbs to make the text more interesting. Cross out the wrong word.**

The next day Amy and Derek went on a **fantastic** • **fantastically** New Delhi tour. "We can **easy** • **easily** see the sights on foot," Derek said. They saw many **beautiful** • **beautifully** monuments. After a few hours Amy was **awful** • **awfully** tired. "Can we **quick** • **quickly** go back to the hotel, please?" But Derek wanted to see the Taj Mahal.

● **4** (WRITING) **Now write the complete story of Amy and Derek's trip. Find a nice ending. You can use the ideas here or your own ideas. Write 12 sentences or 100 words.**
55/3

go to India | lots of sights | hot | cows are important | interesting sights | very tired | Taj Mahal | more tourists | wait in a queue | take a break | pool in the hotel | Indian food

Use the simple past and check the word order.

5 **Check step 3 for writing skills on page 55 in your book. Take notes and talk to a partner.**
55/3

What went well? ______

What can you do better? ______

Which tips did you get? ______

Hör-Dateien online wz68ud

Discover South Africa

62/2

1 What do you know about South Africa?

a) Read the texts on pages 62 and 63 in your book and complete the sentences for each picture.

a) South Africa has three capitals: ____________________

____

b) ______ % of the population are African, ______ % are European.

c) Cape Town is famous for a mountain called ____________________

____________________.

a) In 1994 Nelson Mandela became ____________ of South Africa.

b) He was the first ____________ South African president.

c) Apartheid separated ____________________.

a) The largest park in South Africa is ____________________.

b) It has an area of nearly 20,000 ____________________.

c) You can go on safari in the national parks and see wild animals like ____________________.

b) Read the texts on pages 62 and 63 in your book again and tick ✓ right or wrong.

	right		wrong	
1. South Africa became independent from Africa in 1934.	☐	t	☐	r
2. In the same year apartheid ended in South Africa.	☐	o	☐	a
3. Apartheid ended 60 years later.	☐	n	☐	u
4. You can listen to eleven official languages in South Africa.	☐	g	☐	r
5. Rich South African people live in townships.	☐	d	☐	e
6. Not many South African children finish high school.	☐	r	☐	e

The letters behind your right answers make a word for a typical job in South Africa: ____________

65/4 1 **Write the words for the definitions.**

1. to stop a bike or a car
2. another word for 'hurt'
3. the opposite of 'poor'
4. the opposite of 'to start'
5. a little piece of information
6. If you want to drive a car, you need a …
7. When two cars crash, there is an …

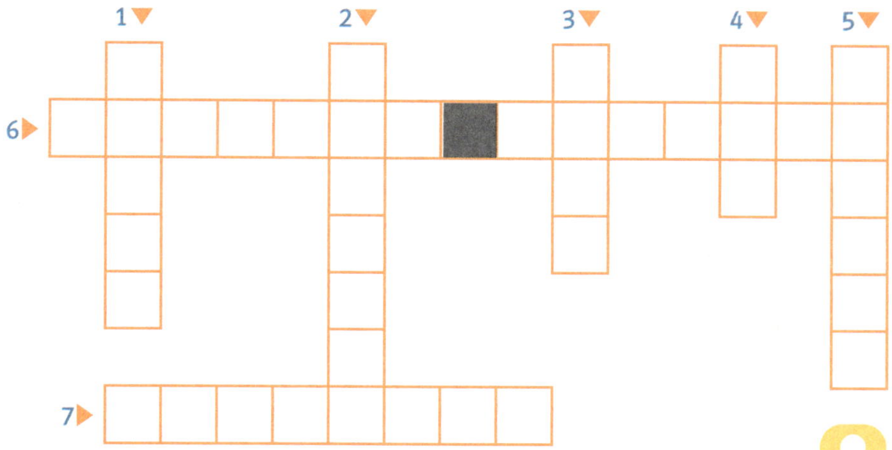

8 65/5 2 (LISTENING) **Listen to the dialogue at the police station. Complete the sentences with the right information from the boxes. There are more answers than you need.**

green and grey | stolen her wallet | found her credit card | her address | 800 rand | 800 euros | her friend's name | find the wallet | find the friend | small and grey | cellphone | cash card | credit card | Durban Hotel near the beach | Luxor Hotel on Alton Road

1. Cathy thinks that someone has ______________________ when she was at the beach.
2. The police officer wants to know her name and ______________________.
3. Cathy is staying at the ______________________.
4. Her wallet is ______________________.
5. What was in Cathy's wallet? ______________________ in currency
6. What else was in her wallet? Her ______________ and her ______________.

65/6 3 (SOUNDS) **Read, say and listen.**

a) The words below are spelt with the letter 'a' but they sound different. Read them, say them and write them in the right group.

all | brake | crash | fast | glass | man | station | tall

/ɔ:/ salt	/eɪ/ crazy	/æ/ bang	/ɑ:/ large
______	______	______	______
______	______	______	______

9 b) Listen to the words and check your group of words. Then say the words again.

4 Complete the text with the verbs in the simple past.

66/7

At home, Nicole's mum wants to know all about the accident in Durban.

Nicole's mum: Oh Nicole, good that you are back home. I (1) ____________ (hear) about that accident on the radio. What (2) ____________ (be) it like? (3) ____________ (be) you very scared?

Nicole: Mum, relax! It (4) ____________ (not be) that bad. I was talking to my friend Cebile when the accident (5) ____________ (happen). A car (6) ____________ (hit) our bus. All the glass at the front of the bus (7) ____________ (fall) out. Then we (8) ____________ (have) to go to the police station. So we (9) ____________ (not go) to the cricket match. And I (10) ____________ (not spend) the money that you (11) ____________ (give) me.

Nicole's mum: (12) ____________ (be) anybody hurt?

Nicole: Yes, I think the bus driver (13) ____________ (be) injured and taken to hospital.

5 Look at the picture. What was happening yesterday?

66/8

a) What was everybody doing? Use the past progressive with these verbs.

1. Yesterday afternoon a dog *was taking* (take) a hot dog at the market.
2. The man with the red T-shirt ____________ (sell) bananas.
3. The tall woman with the pink dress ____________ (look) and ____________ (smile) at him.
4. Two young girls ____________ (eat) chicken.

5. A girl and a boy were tired and they ____________ (think) about sitting down.

b) Look at the picture again. What was not happening? Use the past progressive of these verbs or use your own ideas.

not sell | not wear | not buy | not eat | not look | wasn't | weren't

1. *The dog wasn't looking at the bananas.*
2. The man with the red T-shirt ____________
3. The woman with the pink dress ____________
4. The girls ____________
5. ____________

67/9

6 (SPEAKING) What were you doing? Talk to a partner.

Ask the questions to a partner. Then your partner asks you. Write down your answers. You can use some of these verbs or your own ideas.

study | do homework | listen to music | play | wear | work | sit | read | watch

1. What were you doing yesterday afternoon? ______________________
2. What were you wearing? ______________________
3. Were you studying? ______________________
4. What was your brother or sister doing? ______________________
5. What were your parents doing? ______________________
6. Who was sitting next to you in class? ______________________

67/10

7 While and when – put in the simple past or the past progressive.

while + past progressive, when + simple past

Yesterday evening John (1) *was driving* (drive) home quite fast when suddenly he (2) ______________ (see) a rabbit. The rabbit was running across the street when John (3) ______________ (try) to brake. Suddenly another car crashed into John's car while the little rabbit (4) ______________ (look) back from the other side of the street. Luckily, nobody was hurt. While John and the driver (5) ______________ (talk) about the accident, the rabbit ran back into the wood. John's phone rang while he (6) ______________ (write) down the driver's address. They (7) ______________ (wait) for the police when suddenly a second rabbit crossed the street.

67/10

8 What is it in English? Use the past progressive.

1. Frage einen Freund oder eine Freundin, was er oder sie gestern nachmittag gemacht hat. (do)

   ____

2. Sage, dass du den ganzen Nachmittag dein Fahrrad repariert hast. (repair)

   ____

3. Frage den Freund oder die Freundin, wo er oder sie gestern den neuen Film gesehen hat. (watch)

   ____

4. Sage, dass du gestern nichts angeschaut hast. (not watch anything)

   ____

69/2 1 Facts about Miriam Makeba

Complete the sentences and do the crossword.

1. Miriam Makeba is a great South African … model.
2. She was a South African … and songwriter.
3. Miriam Makeba fought against … .
4. Black people had to live in … at that time.
5. When she left her country, the … took away her passport.
6. So she couldn't go back home to … Africa.
7. Her life has been an … for a long time.
8. She has … a lot for her country.

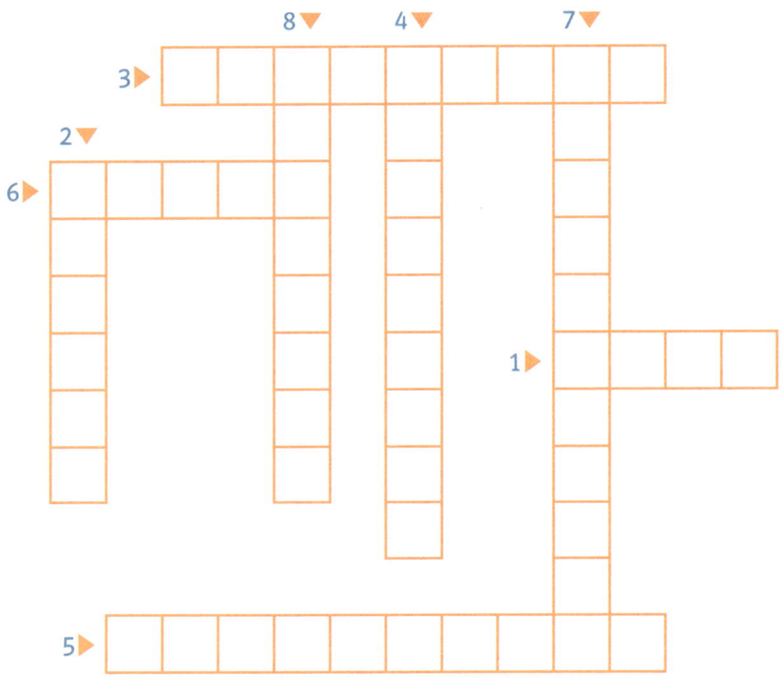

10 69/5 2 (LISTENING) Listen to Nelson Mandela's life and complete the text.

1. Nelson Mandela lived from 1918 until ____________________.
2. In 1964 he and his group __________________________ government buildings.
3. Mandela spent ________________________ of his life in prison.
4. In ____________________ Mandela left _____________________ and worked together with President de Klerk.
5. They wanted to end apartheid __________________________.
6. In 1994 Nelson Mandela became the first ____________________ president.
7. He started a _______________________ for people with AIDS.
8. The charity's name was 46664, his prison _______________________ on Robben Island.

70/6 ↗ **3** **How long have you done it? Since or for?**

Write down the words in the right group.

2003 | a long time | Sunday | 5 p.m. | two weeks | 1st April | three hours | a year | yesterday | some days

since bei Zeitpunkten:
since 3 o'clock
for bei Zeitspannen:
for a day

Since	For
______	______
______	______
______	______
______	______
______	______

70/7 ↗ 71/8 ↗ **4** **Use the present perfect.**

a) Complete the sentences with the present perfect and write since or for.

1. Sister Anne ______ (live) in South Africa ______ 2020.
2. She ______ (work) in a hospital near Pretoria ______ January.
3. She helps people who ______ (not see) a doctor ______ a long time.
4. AIDS ______ (be) a serious problem in South Africa ______ many years.
5. Anne: There are lots of problems, but it is great to see what South Africans ______ (achieve) ______ 1994.

b) Make questions with the present perfect. Add a short answer.

1. ______ your parents ever ______ (be) to South Africa? ______
2. ______ you ever ______ (meet) any people from South Africa? ______
3. ______ you ever ______ (listen) to South African music? ______
4. ______ you and your friends ever ______ (hear) about AIDS? ______
5. ______ you and your friends ever ______ (talk) about charities? ______
6. ______ your teacher ever ______ (organize) a flea market for the poor people in Africa? ______
7. ______ you ever ______ (bake) a cake for a friend? ______

74/2 1 (MEDIATION) Pass on information from signs in a hospital.

1
BEFORE YOUR VISIT:
WASH YOUR HANDS, PLEASE.

2
EMERGENCY
Adults & Children

3
Visitor information
No more than three visitors
per patient at a time.

Im Urlaub in Südafrika musst du wegen einer Verletzung ins Krankenhaus zur Behandlung. Deine Eltern können nicht gut Englisch sprechen. Hilf ihnen, die Informationen auf den Schildern zu verstehen. Beantworte ihre Fragen in Stichpunkten auf Deutsch.

1. Was sollst du vor einem Krankenbesuch tun?

   ____

2. Wohin geht es für Erwachsene und Kinder, wenn sie nach rechts gehen?

   ____

3. Was steht auf dem Schild Besucherinformation?

   ____

74/2 2 (MEDIATION) Pass on the visitor information.

Visitor information

1. Don't bring food or drinks. Patients get their food from the hospital.
2. Flowers are not allowed.
3. Smoking is not allowed in the whole building.
4. It's best not to sit on the patient's bed. Use a chair.
5. Do not use the patient's toilet. Use the hospital's public toilet.
6. Visitors shouldn't stay longer than 20 minutes.

Beim Besuch eines kranken Freundes in einem Krankenhaus in Kapstadt liest du diese Hinweise. Ergänze die Informationen auf Deutsch.

1. Man soll kein ______________ mitbringen, weil die Patienten ihr Essen ______________ bekommen.
2. ______________ sind ebenfalls nicht gestattet.
3. Im gesamten Gebäude ist das ______________ verboten.
4. Man soll sich nicht auf ______________ setzen, sondern auf ______________.
5. Man soll nicht die ______________ benutzen, sondern die ______________ im Krankenhaus.
6. Es wird empfohlen, pro Besuch ______________ 20 Minuten zu bleiben.

73/4

1 (READING) Young people in South Africa

Read the text.

My name is Mufasa and I'm 21 years old. I was lucky when three years ago I got a job in the office of an organization called Save South Africa's Wildlife.

One day I want to work as a guide in a national park. That's my big dream. When tourists go on safari, I would like to tell them about the problems wildlife has and also show them the beautiful national parks. Kruger National Park is a good example of how to protect wildlife.

Today, South Africa is home to more than 24,000 elephants. I think elephants are amazing. Do you know why I like them so much? A poster in my office says: "Elephants never give up their family or friends, but man does."

The situation in South Africa is not always easy for young black people. I'm sad when my friends say that they want to leave South Africa. My older sister also left our country two years ago. She went to Germany to study. She fell in love with a boy from Munich. Now they have invited my family over because they want to marry in September. Isn't that great? My parents saved all their money for the journey. We've never been to Europe. This will be our first time.

● 2 Answer the questions about Mufasa's life.

73/4

1. Why was Mufasa lucky?

____

____

2. What is his dream?

____

3. What would Mufasa like to do as a guide in a national park?

____

4. Why does Mufasa like elephants so much?

____

5. Why is he sometimes sad?

____

6. Why will Mufasa visit Germany in September?

____

7. Has Mufasa been to Europe before?

____

8. How do you know that Mufasa is happy about the trip to Germany?

____

Lösungen online i5z2in

___/4P Ziel 1: Ich kann Informationen über Südafrika verstehen.

→p.48/1

South Africa is the most southern country on the African continent. It has a coast along the Atlantic and Indian Oceans and has borders with six other African countries.
The people of South Africa are proud of their country with its beautiful landscapes and amazing wildlife. Many tourists come to take part in safaris in one of the many national parks or to enjoy the country's beautiful beaches. Since apartheid ended, South Africa has been known as the 'rainbow nation' because of its many different languages and traditions. There are rich and poor people in South Africa. However, many poor black people in townships and in the country live without sanitation or electricity.

Tick ✓ the right facts.

1. South Africa has six coasts along the Atlantic Ocean. ☐
2. South Africa has borders with six other African countries. ☐
3. South Africa has beautiful beaches and lots of national parks. ☐
4. South Africa doesn't have many tourists who take part in safaris. ☐
5. Different traditions and languages make South Africa a rainbow nation. ☐
6. Different weather conditions make a lot of rainbows in South Africa. ☐
7. Most poor black people don't live in townships but in the country. ☐
8. A lot of poor black people live in houses without electricity. ☐

___/9P Ziel 2: Ich kann über einen Unfall sprechen.

→p.48/2

Use the words in brackets to complete the text. Change the words if you need to.

E-MAIL

Hi Marie,

Guess what! A car (1) ____________ (crash) into our bus yesterday. Piet (2) ____________ (be) injured. He (3) ____________ (be) OK now. It all happened so (4) ____________ (quick)! I sent a message to Jade while we (5) ____________ (wait). Then we (6) ____________ (have) to go to the police station. The police officer, Riah Nkosi, was very (7) ____________ (friend). We answered all her (8) ____________ (question). My parents (9) ____________ (take) me home an hour later.

See you tomorrow.

Bye,

Louise

__/10P Ziel 3: Ich kann einen Text über mein Vorbild schreiben.

→p.49/3

a) Match the right sentence parts.

1. I admire
2. He fought for
3. He spent 27 years
4. Mandela became the first
5. He also started a charity
6. I think he really

a. changed the world.
b. in prison.
c. black president of South Africa in 1994.
d. Nelson Mandela very much.
e. black people's rights.
f. to raise money for people with AIDS.

b) Write four sentences about a person you admire. You can use these words or your own ideas.

friendly | nice | have fun | good at | help | great friend | have time | listen to | laugh

____

____

__/4P Ziel 4: Ich kann einen Text über das Leben junger Menschen verstehen.

→p.49/4

Read the text on page 45 again. Answer the questions. Write short answers.

1. Did Mufasa get a job as a guide in a national park? ____________
2. Is the Kruger National Park a good example of how to protect wildlife? ____________
3. Do more than 24,000 elephants live in South Africa? ____________
4. Is the situation in South Africa easy for young black people? ____________

__/6P Ziel 5: Ich kann Informationen in einem Krankenhaus weitergeben.

→p.49/5

1
DO NOT ENTER!
Ask a nurse
if you want to see a baby.

2
QUIET AREA
DO NOT USE PHONES
IN THIS AREA

3
Visiting hours
Mon–Fri 10:00 – 11:30 a.m.
Mon–Sun 2:00 – 4:00 p.m.
Children must be with an adult.

Lies, was auf den Schildern steht und vervollständige die Angaben auf Deutsch.

1. Betreten verboten. Man soll ____________

   ____
2. Ruhezone. Hier soll man ____________
3. Besuchszeiten: ____________: 10–11:30 Uhr,

   ____________: 14–16 Uhr, Kinder müssen ____________

Lösungen online
i5z2in

○ Ziel 1: Ich kann Informationen über Südafrika verstehen.

South Africa is the most southern country in Africa. It has a long coast and borders with six other African countries.
The people of South Africa are proud of their country. They love the beautiful landscapes and the amazing wildlife. Many tourists come to go on safaris in one of the many national parks or spend time on the beautiful beaches.
Since apartheid ended, South Africa has been known as the 'rainbow nation' because there are so many different languages and traditions.
There are rich and poor people in South Africa. Many poor black people live in townships and in the country. They often live without electricity.

Read the text and complete the sentences. You don't need all the words.

prisons • townships • safaris • borders • wildlife • proud of • apartheid

1. South Africa has ____________________ with six other African countries.
2. South African people are very ____________________ their country.
3. Tourists in South Africa like to go on ____________________ in one of the national parks.
4. People call South Africa a 'rainbow nation' since ____________________ ended.
5. A lot of poor black people live in the country or in ____________________.

○ Ziel 2: Ich kann über einen Unfall sprechen.

Circle the right words.

E-MAIL

Hi Marie,

Guess what! A car (1) **crashes** • **crashed** into our bus yesterday.

Piet (2) **was** • **were** injured. He (3) **is** • **was** OK now.

It all happened so (4) **quick** • **quickly**!

I sent a message to Jade while we (5) **were waiting** • **waited**.

Then we (6) **have** • **had** to go to the police station.

The police officer, Riah Nkosi, was very (7) **friend** • **friendly**.

We answered all her (8) **question** • **questions**.

My parents (9) **take** • **took** me home an hour later.

See you tomorrow.

Bye,

Louise

○ **Ziel 3: Ich kann einen Text über mein Vorbild schreiben.**

Complete the text with the correct verbs. Watch the tenses!

think | raise | spend | admire | fight | become

1. I ____________________ Nelson Mandela very much.
2. He ____________________ for black people's rights.
3. He ____________________ 27 years in prison.
4. Mandela ____________________ the first black president in South Africa in 1994.
5. He also started a charity to ____________________ money for people with AIDS.
6. I ____________________ he really changed the world.

○ **Ziel 4: Ich kann einen Text über das Leben junger Menschen verstehen.**

Read the text on page 45 again. Cross out the wrong statements.

1. Mufasa got a job **as a guide in a national park** • **in an office of an organization**.
2. The Kruger National Park **is a good** • **is not a good** example of how to protect wildlife.
3. More than 24,000 elephants live **in South Africa** • **in the Kruger National Park**.
4. Young black people **go to** • **want to leave** South Africa because it is not easy for them there.

○ **Ziel 5: Ich kann Informationen in einem Krankenhaus weitergeben.**

1
DO NOT ENTER!
Ask a nurse
if you want to see a baby.

2
QUIET AREA
DO NOT USE PHONES
IN THIS AREA

3
Visiting hours
Mon–Fri 10:00 – 11:30 a.m.
Mon–Sun 2:00 – 4:00 p.m.
Children must be with an adult.

Lies, was auf den Schildern steht und beantworte die Fragen kurz auf Deutsch.

1. Wann soll man eine Krankenschwester fragen? ____________________
2. Warum soll man hier keine Handys benutzen? ____________________
3. Unter welcher Bedingung dürfen Kinder Patienten besuchen?

____

How to pass on information

81/1 **1 Pass on information.**

Gib die unterschiedlichen Satzanfänge wieder.

1. Meine Tante fragt, ob … My aunt asks if …
2. Die Rangerin weist darauf hin, dass … ______
3. Meine Tante möchte gerne wissen, warum … ______
4. Der Polizist erklärt, dass … ______
5. Ein Tourist erkundigt sich, wo … ______

● **2 Tips and tricks**

81/2

Ein deutscher Ausdruck kann oft mit verschiedenen Worten erklärt werden. Übe, dich unterschiedlich auszudrücken. Ordne die deutschen Ausdrücke richtig zu und finde englische Verben dafür.

sagen | schreiben | etwas tun | etwas sehr mögen | wissen wollen | fragen, bitten | verboten sein | an etwas denken | jemanden sehr mögen | sich interessieren für | auf etwas aufpassen | wichtig sein | nicht erlaubt sein

Deutscher Ausdruck		
etwas übertragen	– sagen, schreiben	– say, write
etwas beachten	– ______ – ______	– ______ – ______
nicht tun dürfen	– ______ – ______	– ______ – ______
am Herzen liegen	– ______ – ______	– ______ – ______
sich erkundigen	– ______ – ______	– ______ – ______

81/4 **3 Ask for help. Write the English sentences.**

1. Könnten Sie bitte etwas langsamer sprechen? ______
2. Können Sie das bitte noch einmal erklären? ______
3. Ich bin nicht sicher, was Sie meinen. ______
4. Das habe ich nicht verstanden. ______

Ein zweisprachiges Wörterbuch in Printform ist für die gesamte schriftliche Prüfung erlaubt.

Hör-Dateien online wz68ud

A Listening Comprehension (Hörverstehen)

11 **1 Listen to a teenager from South Africa. Tick ✓ right or wrong. There is an example (0.) at the beginning.**

Akani

	right	wrong
0. More than a million people live in Soweto.	✓	☐
1. Nelson Mandela is a famous person from Soweto too.	☐	☐
2. A lot of people say townships are safe.	☐	☐
3. Rich people love the community.	☐	☐
4. Akani lives near his family.	☐	☐
5. Everybody leaves their door open so they can visit each other.	☐	☐
6. He often plays games in the street with his friends.	☐	☐
7. Akani's mum has a little restaurant in the area.	☐	☐
8. Akani sometimes helps in the restaurant's kitchen.	☐	☐

12 **2 Listen to Akani. Write short answers. There is an example (0.) at the beginning.**

0. How many brothers and sisters does Akani have? *Two sisters and one brother.*
1. Where does Akani's family get water from? ______
2. What job does everyone hate doing? ______
3. Where can Akani watch rugby matches? ______
4. Where does Akani's dad work? ______
5. How does Akani get to school? ______
6. What are they going to do at Akani's school? *Work on* ______
7. What other problems are there in the townships? ______
8. What does Akani love doing in his free time? *He loves* ______

B Use of English (Sprachgebrauch)

1 South Africa

Complete the sentences with the right words. There is an example (0.) at the beginning.

0. South Africa has beautiful landscapes and amazing w i l d l i f e.
1. A lot of poor people in South Africa live in t _ _ _ _ _ _ _ _.
2. They often don't have sanitation or e _ _ _ _ _ _ _ _ _ _.
3. People like Miriam Makeba are r _ _ _ m _ _ _ _ _ for many South Africans.
4. Miriam Makeba achieved a lot for South Africa. She fought against a _ _ _ _ _ _ _ _.
5. When you don't have a job you are u _ _ _ _ _ _ _ _ _.
6. Organizations which help people with problems or diseases are called c _ _ _ _ _ _ _ _.

2 Facts about South Africa

Read some facts about South Africa. There is one mistake in each sentence. Circle ◯ the mistakes and correct them. There is an example (0.) at the beginning.

	correct word
0. South Africa (become) independent in 1934.	(0) became
1. Their are three capitals in South Africa: Pretoria, Cape Town, Bloemfontein.	(1) ______
2. Cape Town is famous four Table Mountain.	(2) ______
3. South Africa is called a rainbow nation because there are much different languages and traditions.	(3) ______
4. Apartheid started after independence and separated black and right people.	(4) ______
5. Apartheid ended in 1994 why Nelson Mandela became president.	(5) ______
6. Mandela were the first black president of South Africa.	(6) ______
7. In the national parks in South Africa you can see elephants and lion.	(7) ______
8. The larger national park in South Africa is Kruger National Park.	(8) ______
9. Lots of poor people life in townships or near the cities.	(9) ______
10. Poor people in South Africa often have not water at home.	(10) ______

3 On safari in a national park

Read the blog about a safari. Complete it with the right words from the box. You don't need all the words. There is an example (0) at the beginning.

a • afraid • always • amazing • an • because of • damage • driving licence • enjoyed • from • front • guide • hot • in • jump • lying • never • new • old • on ✓ • which • while • who • with • worked

INTERNET

Hi everyone!

I went (0) _on_ ________ safari with my family yesterday. It was (1) ________________. You aren't allowed to drive alone in the national park (2) ________________ the wild animals. So a (3) ________________ went with us. At first she told us that she was (4) ________________ there. You could see how much she (5) ________________ her job. She was a great guide and (6) ____________ good driver. She wanted to show us lots of wild animals, (7) ________________ wasn't easy. However, we saw a lion (8) ________________ under a tree, and in the distance we saw some elephants drinking water (9) ________________ a lake. There were even two small elephants (10) ________________ them. The tour was a great experience I will (11) ________________ forget. What (12) ____________ adventure!

4 Table Mountain in South Africa

Read the text about Table Mountain. Circle ◯ the words that fit the sentences. There is an example (0) at the beginning.

Table Mountain is a famous sight (0) **at** • **(near)** • **on** Cape Town in South Africa. It has a flat top, just (1) **when** • **like** • **how** a table. That is (2) **why** • **what** • **who** it is called a 'table-top' mountain. You (3) **saw** • **have seen** • **can see** Table Mountain from everywhere in Cape Town. Lots of visitors take the cable car (4) **to** • **on** • **by** the top or even walk up the mountain. Table Mountain is (5) **between** • **in** • **under** Table Mountain National Park and the mountain is more (6) **as** • **then** • **than** 1,000 metres (7) **high** • **great** • **big**. Table Mountain in South Africa is the (8) **more** • **most** • **best** famous table-top mountain in the world.

C Reading Comprehension (Leseverstehen)

Amahle's story

Apartheid was all I knew. My dad, a teacher, died during a protest. A police officer killed him when I was a baby. My family didn't talk about politics and we tried to stay out of trouble.
Our house was in a black township. We had no electricity and no sanitation. My mum went to work every day, and my grandma and aunts helped to look after my brother, sister and me. We all had to leave school and work as soon as we were 13 because we needed the money for our family.
I wanted to go to university, but as soon as I left school, I worked in a white family's kitchen. I was angry at the world. I thought all my problems were because of white people. That's how I felt.

It was early February in 1990 when we heard the news on TV. Apartheid was going to end. We celebrated all night. But things didn't change very quickly; it took a lot of time to end apartheid. However, I left my job in the kitchen and got a job in a small restaurant in a nice part of town.

One day, an old white man came in. I knew his face from TV. This man was an important police officer in the apartheid system. He was the man who told the police to attack the protesters when my dad died. I got so angry! How could he sit there and peacefully eat in a restaurant? Didn't he remember the dead people? My dad? I put the plate on the table in front of him, looked into his grey eyes and said, "You killed my father." I didn't wait for an answer. I just turned and went back into the kitchen.

When the restaurant closed, he was still there. "Can I talk to you?" he asked. I sat down opposite him. "I'm sorry," he said. We spoke for an hour. I told him about my mum and about my life. He told me how he began trying to stop police violence against black people. I didn't know what to think. But then I thought I was as bad as the police officers if I couldn't look to the future instead of looking to the past.

When he was ready to leave, he held out his hand to me. I took it in mine and looked him in the eyes again. "It's OK," I told him. It felt good to say those words. I don't know if my mum or dad would have done the same, but I knew it was what I needed to do so I could live my life.

1 Tick the right meaning of these words from the text. There is an example (0.) at the beginning.

0. tried (line 3)		1. left (line 9 and 12)		2. turned (line 18)		3. live (line 25)	
a) versuchten	☑	a) links	☐	a) bog ab	☐	a) live, Live-	☐
b) prüften	☐	b) verließ	☐	b) wurde	☐	b) wohnen	☐
c) probierten aus	☐	c) übrig	☐	c) drehte mich um	☐	c) leben	☐

2 Read Amahle's story again. Answer the questions. Write short answers. There is an example (0.) at the beginning.

0. Where did Amahle live? *In a house in a black township.*
1. Who supported Amahle's mother? ______
2. Why did Amahle know the old white man's face? ______
3. What did Amahle and the man talk about? ______

______
4. How did Amahle feel after her talk with the police officer? ______

D Text Production (Schreiben)

1 **Betrachte die Bilder und schreibe eine Fortführung der Geschichte auf Englisch. Was erlebt Robins Familie noch auf der Safari? Nutze die Ideen aus der Box oder denke dir selbst etwas aus. Schreibe ungefähr 100 Wörter oder 12 Sätze.**

Ideas: more wild animals • something wrong with the wheel • ranger must call service station • have to wait for … • hot and dry • empty bottles • not a good idea to take a shower like the elephants • extra bottles of water in a box under the seat • happy • learn the lesson • back at the hotel

When Robin and his family went on safari in Kruger National Park they saw some elephants near some water. It was really hot and the elephants used the water to cool down. So Robin and his sister had an idea: they took their water bottles and emptied them over their heads. What a wonderful feeling! They thought, "Elephants have the best ideas." A little later …

E Mediation (Sprachmittlung)

Du träumst davon, nach deinem Schulabschluss mit deiner Familie nach Südafrika zu reisen. Du informierst dich im Internet und findest einen Reisebericht über Südafrika.

INTERNET

Travelling to South Africa? Take a look at my tips first.

If you travel to South Africa, you'll find great things that you wouldn't do at home. How about river rafting or paragliding in an amazing South African landscape? A safari or whale watching is also a must – something you can't (usually) do at home.

Travelling with children

If you are travelling with children, take their original birth certificates with you. Copies are not accepted.

Valuables

Your suitcases should be locked when you check them in at the airport. It's best to keep all your valuables in your hand luggage and don't carry too much money with you. You don't want to lose anything, do you?

Where to stay

Staying in a beautiful apartment is a good alternative to an expensive hotel. Look here for tips on how to book an apartment in South Africa. Don't walk around by yourself in the cities at night. Stay in a group and use busy streets.

Cape Town

Take your time in this great city. You should go to the Waterfront with its fantastic sights, shops and restaurants. It is a safe area. Of course, there are lots of great places and things to see, but make sure you don't miss Table Mountain.

Table Mountain

Even if you visit in the summer, it can get cold – it is a mountain. Make sure you wear warm clothes or take an extra sweatshirt with you. Book the cable car to the top online as there is often a two-hour wait at busy times. It only takes two hours to walk to the top – a good alternative for active people.

Nachdem du den Reisebericht gelesen hast, sprichst du mit deinen Eltern. Sie haben einige Fragen, die du mit Hilfe der neuen Informationen beantworten kannst.

Deine Eltern	Du
	Nach meinem Schulabschluss würde ich gerne mit euch nach Südafrika reisen. Das ist mein ganz großer Traum.
Was findest du denn an Südafrika so toll? Warum möchtest du da unbedingt hin?	(1) ____________________
OK. Aber dürfen wir da überhaupt mit Kind einreisen? Du bist doch dann erst 17.	(2) ____________________
Ich mache mir ein bisschen Sorgen wegen der Wertsachen und wegen des Geldes. Wie verhält man sich am besten?	(3) ____________________
Und wo wohnen wir? Hotels sind ganz schön teuer für eine ganze Familie.	(4) ____________________
Kann es in den Städten nicht auch gefährlich sein?	(5) ____________________
Welche Stadt wäre denn ideal für uns?	(6) ____________________
Table Mountain klingt gut. Wie kommt man da hoch?	(7) ____________________ *Wir sind ja sportlich. Was meint ihr?*
Hört sich interessant an, schauen wir mal. Du hast dich schon gut informiert!	

Hör-Dateien online wz68ud

News from New Zealand

88/2 **1** **Read the texts on pages 88 and 89 in your book. Then read the texts next to the pictures. Two pieces of information for each picture are wrong. Underline and correct them.**

Facts and numbers
New Zealand is 1,000 miles away from Australia, in the Atlantic Ocean. Fewer than five million people live there. About a third of the people in New Zealand live in its biggest city, Auckland. New Zealand's capital, however, is Christchurch.

Nature
New Zealand has two main islands with beautiful landscapes. They are part of the 'Ring of Parts'. In this area around the Pacific Ocean there are many landscapes. Earthquakes often happen there.

The Maori
Around 1250 the Maori people came to New Zealand. They came from rocks in the Pacific Ocean. Today English and Maori are official populations in New Zealand.

Free time and sport
Rugby is the national organization in New Zealand. New Zealand's rugby team is very good. Rugby has become a popular free-time activity in New Zealand. Many people are volunteers of sports clubs.

88/2 **2** (WRITING) **Which picture about New Zealand do you like best? Say why.**

Choose a picture from ex.1 and write two or three sentences to say why you like it.

91/4 ↗ **1** Complete the crossword with the right words.

1. the paper which you get when you leave school
2. the person who gives you a job and pays you
3. a piece of paper where you fill in personal information
4. another word for help
5. A careers advisor can help you to find out about your … for a job.
6. the place where a mechanic often works
7. The time that will come is your …
8. another word for tip

Finish the sentence with the word for 9.

9. Before you choose a career, you can ________________ a job suitability test.

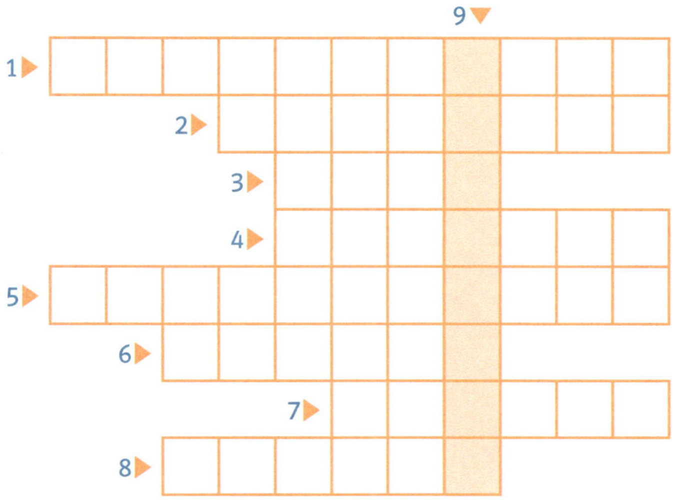

13 92/6 ↗ **2** (LISTENING) Listen and fill in the table.

Mrs Thompson has a restaurant. She is looking for a chef. At the careers day she is talking to some young people. Complete her notes.

Name	Jill ________
Experience	helps in ________
Qualities and skills	can ________ has no problem ________
Train as a/ Work as a	________ because she ________

❀ 92/6 ↗ **3** (WRITING) A careers day at your school

Make some notes for an interview with a careers advisor. Complete the form.

Name	________
Experience	________
Qualities and skills Hobbies	________ ________ ________
Train/Work as a/Work in	________

92/7 ## 4 What are Ella and Liam going to do? What are they not going to do?

Read the sentences. Use the correct form of be and going to or not going to.

1. Liam ______________________________ (apply) to different tourist information centres.
2. He ______________________________ (not do) a job suitability test. He has done one already.
3. Liam and Ella ______________________________ (get) some experience before they decide on a job.
4. Ella ______________________________ (not stay) at her aunt's hairdressing salon.
5. She ______________________________ (apply) to a different hairdresser.
6. Ella and Liam ______________________________ (find out) more information about the job fair next month. They want to go there.
7. Liam: I ______________________________ (phone) some companies next week too.
8. Liam ______________________________ (not work) as a mechanic in his dad's garage.

93/9 ## 5 Write questions and answer them.

a) Liam's grandfather is talking to Liam's father. Find the right word order and write his questions.

1. in your garage • why • work • going to • isn't • Liam

   Why isn't ______________________________

2. do • is • Liam • going to • when he finishes school • what

   ____

3. who • as a mechanic • is • work for you • going to

   ____

4. are you • in a few years • with the garage • going to • what • do

   ____

b) What could Liam's dad answer? Use the words in the boxes or your own ideas.

not like working with machines | apply for a job in tourism | not know yet | sell it

1. ______________________________
2. ______________________________
3. ______________________________
4. ______________________________

93/10

6 What is the right job for them?

Look at the pictures. They can help you to find out what the young people are going to do. Write down complete sentences. Use the words in brackets.

1. Eliza loves giving support and likes working in a kindergarten or a hospital. (train)
   She is going to train as a nurse.
2. Meg likes writing computer programs. (be • computer programmer)
3. Tom loves fashion and cutting hair. (train)
4. Nick likes working with plants and animals. (work • pet shop or garden centre)
5. Laura loves working in a team. (apply for a job • office)

93/10

7 (SPEAKING) I am the right person for this job.

Choose a job you would like to do. Why are you the right person for this job? Make notes. Work in groups of four and present your ideas to the others. Here are some ideas.

chef · farmer · mechanic · police officer · receptionist · shop assistant · vet's assistant · ...

communication skills · computer skills · confident · flexible · calm in difficult situations · quick · reliable · ...

work with machines · communicate with · work in a team · help people · speak English · ...

Use a verb with -ing after 'I'm good at' or after 'I like'.

One day I would like to be a

I can

I have

I'm good at

I like

95/3 ↗

1 Complete the sentences with the right words.

1. Shop assistants help people find the right _ _ _ _ _ [c] _ _ in a store.
2. Shop assistants also fill the _ [ ] _ _ _ _ _.
3. People who buy things in a supermarket are called _ _ _ _ _ _ [ ] _ _.
4. Many supermarkets buy their products from _ _ [ ] _ _ suppliers.
5. People who _ _ [ ] _ part in an internship programme are called interns.
6. Many supermarkets _ [ ] _ _ _ _ food to local charities.
7. Giving food to local charities helps to _ _ _ [ ] _ _ food waste.
8. Supermarkets often offer summer jobs for _ _ _ _ _ _ [ ] _.

Fill in the letters from 1.–8. to find a new word.

1	2	3	4	5	6	7	8
c							

95/3 ↗

2 Put in the right verbs. You don't need all the verbs.

is told · was born · were born · is made · are called · are sold · are offered

1. A lot of summer jobs ______________ every year.
2. Your application needs your name, your address and the date when you ______________.
3. Think of different jobs. Bread, for example, ______________ by bakers very early in the morning.
4. People who work in a shop and sell products ______________ shop assistants.

95/4 ↗

3 Circle the right word to complete the sentence.

1. In a supermarket customers pay at the **supplier.** • **checkout.** • **community.**
2. A lot of supermarkets buy their products from **local** • **famous** • **popular** companies.
3. You can apply for **communication** • **a customer service** • **an internship** in the office of a store.
4. Your employer pays you **an intern** • **a salary** • **a retail** for your work.

95/5 ↗

4 (SOUNDS) Read, say and listen.

a) Read and say the words. Write them in the right group.

day · person · name · supplier · my · they · service · turn · write

/aɪ/ buy	/ɜː/ learn	/eɪ/ way

14 b) Listen to the words and check your answers. Then say the words.

5 Read about Grace's internship on page 96 in your book. Answer the questions with the right short answer.

96/7

1. Did Grace do an internship at a computer store? ____________
2. Did other interns work at the company too? ____________
3. Did she have to talk to customers on the phone? ____________
4. Was there a computer in the office? ____________
5. Could she already make appointments? ____________
6. Did she travel to work by train? ____________
7. Was Grace disappointed about her first day at the company? ____________

6 (SPEAKING) Act a dialogue about an internship.

97/8

Partner A

Frage, wo er oder sie das letzte Praktikum gemacht hat.

Where did you do ____________

Partner B

Sage, dass du dein letztes Praktikum in einem Supermarkt gemacht hast.

I did my last internship in ____________

Partner A

Frage, wie viele Stunden er oder sie jeden Tag arbeiten musste.

How many hours ____________

Partner B

Sage, dass du 6 Stunden arbeiten musstest und dass du nach 3 Stunden eine Pause hattest.

____

Partner A

Frage, was er oder sie zur Mittagszeit gemacht hat.

____

Partner B

Sage, dass du mit anderen Praktikanten in ein Café gegangen bist.

____

Partner A

Frage, was er oder sie jeden Tag im Supermarkt getan hat.

____

Partner B

Sage, dass du die Regale aufgefüllt hast und dass du den Kunden geholfen hast, die Produkte zu finden.

____

Partner A

Frage, warum er oder sie sich dieses Praktikum ausgesucht hat.

____

Partner B

Antworte, weil du dich für den Einzelhandel interessierst.

____

97/9 **7** **Read Leah's report. Put in a suitable form of the word in brackets.**

For many weeks I tried my best. I wrote lots of (1) __________ (apply), but no one gave me a chance. Finally I was lucky. My teacher helped me to find an (2) __________ (intern) at a local baker's last April. Every morning I (3) __________ (have to) get up at 2 o'clock. That's quite early, I can tell you. Then my mum (4) __________ (drive) me to the local baker's. I watched how the bakers (5) __________ (make) bread and cakes. Everyone was quite (6) __________ (friend) to me. On the (7) __________ (three) day a baker showed me how to make Bavarian 'Brezeln'. I don't think the job as a baker is easy, but it's great to see what you have (8) __________ (product). I worked there for a week and I liked it. I can really say that my work experience was (9) __________ (interest) for my career. Maybe I (10) __________ (become) a baker myself one day.

8 (WRITING) **Write a report about your last internship. Write about 100 words.**

97/10

You can use these words or use your own ideas.

apply for | internship | working hours per day | name of the company/shop/club | how long? | interesting | great | people there | break | work on the computer | easy job | hard job | what you learned there

Where?
When?
What?
What did you like?

100/1 ## 1 (MEDIATION) A music and drama club in Auckland, New Zealand

INTERNET

Home | News | **Workshops** | Careers | Gallery | Links

Auckland Club of Music and Drama (ACMD)

Looking to act in a film, dance or sing on stage or play a musical instrument? Register now and learn from real music and film experts. We are one of the best in New Zealand.
Workshops for students aged 16–20 who have finished school.

Type of workshop:	**musical instruments like saxophone, guitar, piano, drums etc.**	**drama**	**singing & dancing**
Course starts on: It ends on:	15th February 30th June	2nd January 15th June	1st September 31st December
Number of lessons per month:	20	40	32
Fees due at the end of each month:	NZ $125	NZ $220	NZ $160

We also offer English courses to young people whose first language is not English.
These programmes help you develop important skills like listening, speaking, reading and writing.

Marie hat im Internet einen neuseeländischen Verein gefunden, der interessante Workshops anbietet. Manche Informationen versteht sie nicht so gut. Sie bittet dich um Hilfe.
Beantworte ihre Fragen auf Deutsch. Schlage Wörter, die du nicht erschließen kannst, in einem Wörterbuch nach.

Marie: Der Auckland Club of Music and Drama bietet Workshops an für Leute, die gerne schauspielern oder ein Instrument spielen wollen. Was gibt es noch?

Du: ______________________________

____

Marie: Nehmen sie nur Studenten?

Du: ______________________________

____

Marie: Hier stehen die Daten für die Kurse, aber <u>wie oft</u> findet z. B. der Schauspielkurs statt?

Du: ______________________________

Marie: Die Kursgebühren sind ja ziemlich hoch. Wann muss man die Gebühr dafür bezahlen?

Du: ______________________________

Marie: Ich glaube, mein Englisch ist nicht gut genug für so einen Workshop. Hilft einem jemand?

Du: ______________________________

____

____

99/4 **1** (READING) Read the story. It is adapted from[1] a Maori legend[2].

The legend of Paikea and Ruatapu

The great chief Uenuku lived on the coast of a large island. He had seventy-one sons. Seventy of the sons were chiefs because their mothers came from important families from the island. One of his sons, Ruatapu, however, wasn't a chief. In Uenuku's eyes he wasn't as important as the others because his mother wasn't from a great family. She was just a slave.

One day Uenuku decided to build a great boat for his sons. When it was finished, Uenuku invited all of his sons to see the boat. He combed[3] their hair[4] and made them look like traditional chiefs. After a while they were ready. Only Ruatapu was left.

Ruatapu asked his father, "Are you going to comb my hair?"

Uenuku answered, "I can't. These combs are sacred. They can only be used on chiefs like your brothers."

Ruatapu said, "Am I not your son?"

Uenuku said, "You are. But your mother is a slave so I can't use the combs on your hair."

Ruatapu was very sad and very angry. His father didn't respect him. He felt his life was very unfair. He sat on a beach and made a bad plan. That evening he went down to the ocean to the boat. He climbed inside and cut[5] a small hole in the bottom of the boat.

The next day all the brothers and Ruatapu wanted to take the boat out to sea for the first time. Ruatapu was careful to put his foot over the hole so that no water could come into the boat. The boat was very beautiful and very fast. It was soon far out at sea. When they could no longer see the island, Ruatapu took his foot off the hole. The water quickly came into the boat.

His brothers shouted and tried to throw the water out of the boat, but there was too much. The boat quickly filled with water and sank. Ruatapu held on to a piece of wood. He watched his brothers as they jumped into the water. His youngest brother, Paikea, his father's favourite, tried to swim to the island.

Ruatapu swam after Paikea, but Paikea was not afraid. He called to Ruatapu, "I will not die because the lord[6] of the sea will help me." The lord of the sea heard Paikea say this and sent a great whale to Paikea. Paikea climbed onto its back and rode it towards the island.

Ruatapu was angry. He sent five huge waves after Paikea. But Paikea and the whale were at the island before the waves. The waves went back towards Ruatapu. He was never seen again.

The whale found the other brothers in the water and brought them safely to the island. Paikea's family still live there today and the whale became a smaller island near the coast.

1 adapted from – *angepasst an*; 2 legend – *Legende, Sage*; 3 to comb – *kämmen*; 4 hair – *Haare*; 5 cut – *schneiden*; 6 lord – *Herr*

99/4 **2** Put the events in the right order.

- [ ] Ruatapu was angry and cut a hole in the bottom of the boat.
- [ ] Nobody saw Ruatapu again.
- [1] Chief Uenuku built a great boat for Uenuku's sons.
- [ ] However, the youngest brother Paikea was saved first.
- [ ] The lord of the sea sent Paikea a whale to save him and his brothers.
- [ ] Uenuku didn't comb Ruatapu's hair.
- [ ] Far out at sea the boat sank.

Look up words in a dictionary if you need help.

99/4 ↗ **3** **Read the questions and complete the answers.**

1. Why wasn't Ruatapu as important as the others in Uenuku's eyes?

   His mother was ____________ and not from ______________.

2. What did Uenuku do when the great boat was finished?

   He ____________ all his sons to the boat and combed their hair so that they looked like

   ______________.

3. Why didn't Uenuku comb Ruatapu's hair?

   The combs were ____________ and could only be used on important people like

   ____________.

4. What do you know about the boat made for the sons? Write two facts.

   It was ______________________.

5. Who was Paikea?

   He was Ruatapu's ______________ brother and Uenuku's ______________ son.

6. How did the god of the sea help Paikea?

   He sent him ________________ which brought him safely to ______________.

7. What happened to Ruatapu in the end?

   ____________ knows what happened to Ruatapu.

99/4 ↗ **4** **(SPEAKING) What do you think?**

a) Read the statements. Do you agree or not? Compare your answers with a partner and talk about them.

	I agree.	I don't agree.
1. Uenuku loved all his sons the same way.	☐	☐
2. The chief wasn't nice to Ruatapu. He was his son too.	☐	☐
3. Everybody can understand why Ruatapu was sad and angry.	☐	☐
4. Ruatapu did the right thing when he cut a hole in the boat.	☐	☐
5. The legend's ending is OK because Ruatapu's brothers were saved.	☐	☐
6. It is not possible for a whale to become an island.	☐	☐

You can start like this:
I don't agree with number 1 because the chief didn't respect his son Ruatapu.
What about you?
I agree with number …

b) Wie hat das Sprechen über die Maori-Sage geklappt? ______________________

Was kannst Du noch verbessern? ______________________

Welche Tipps können dir dabei helfen? ______________________

Lösungen online
i9v8fb

___ /5P Ziel 1: Ich kann Informationen über Neuseeland verstehen.

→ p. 70/1

North Island and South Island

New Zealand has two large islands: North Island and South Island. On North Island there are three large volcanoes. Around them you can find lakes, mountains and beaches with black sand. The east coast of North Island has many long beaches with golden sand. Although it is smaller, North Island has the largest cities, like Wellington and Auckland, and the majority of New Zealand's population live there.
South Island is larger than North Island. It has a landscape of huge lakes, rivers and beautiful beaches. The island also has many national parks. On both islands there are big sheep farms. There are about 27 million sheep in New Zealand but only about 4.7 million people.

Complete the sentences.

1. Around the volcanoes on North Island there are ________________, ________________ and beaches with ________________.
2. New Zealand's largest cities are on ________________.
3. Two of the largest cities there are ________________ and ________________.
4. On South Island you can find ________________, ________________, beautiful ________________ and many ________________.
5. ________ million people live in New Zealand and there are about ________________ sheep.

___ /8P Ziel 2: Ich kann über Jobmöglichkeiten und Fähigkeiten sprechen.

→ p. 70/2

Use the correct form of be and going to.

Charlotte: Hi Matt. I (1) ________________ (work) as a receptionist after school. What about you?

Matt: Nick and I (2) ________________ (ask) a careers advisor first. We (3) ________________ (go) to school again. I want to get better qualifications first. Do you know what Ella (4) ________________ (do)?

Charlotte: Yes, she (5) ________________ (be) a hairdresser. What about Cooper and George?

Matt: They (6) ________________ (work) at a garage. They love working with machines. Where (7) ________________ (apply) for a job as a receptionist?

Charlotte: I (8) ________________ (send) my applications to some big hotels. I love big hotels.

___/7P Ziel 3: Ich kann einen Bericht über ein Praktikum schreiben.

→p.71/3

Complete Fiona's report with the right words.

Last June the local supermarket (1) ______________ (offer) jobs for students. I (2) ______________ (be) lucky because I got a job as a shop assistant for four (3) ______________ (week). I worked six hours every day. I filled a lot of (4) ______________ (shelf) and presented the products (5) ______________ (nice). Working at the supermarket was (6) ______________ (interesting) than going to school. But after school I'd like to (7) ______________ (train) as a nurse in a hospital.

___/7P Ziel 4: Ich kann eine Geschichte über verschiedene Generationen verstehen.

→p.71/4

Read the Maori legend on page 66 again. Tick ✓ right, wrong or not in the text.

	right	wrong	not in the text
1. Uenuku had seventy-one sons.	☐	☐	☐
2. Ruatapu's mother was very beautiful.	☐	☐	☐
3. Uenuku told Ruatapu that he wasn't as important as his brothers.	☐	☐	☐
4. Ruatapu was sad, but he accepted his father's decision.	☐	☐	☐
5. Ruatapu's youngest brother Paikea was Uenuku's favourite son.	☐	☐	☐
6. The god of the sea helped Ruatapu with a whale.	☐	☐	☐
7. Later Paikea also had seventy sons.	☐	☐	☐

___/8P Ziel 5: Ich kann Informationen über einen Verein weitergeben.

→p.71/5

Welcome to the Wellington Magicians' Club (WMC)
Arts and traditions of magic since 1999

Our evenings start off with some magic performed by our members. Experienced magicians show you some of their most amazing tricks. There are lots of public performances every year, for example at schools, in kindergartens, in hospitals and at birthday parties. Members under 20 pay a fee of NZ $25. Members over 20 pay NZ $35. The costs for the lessons are included. We meet once a month.
Don't wait, register now.

Lies die Informationen und ergänze die Lücken auf Deutsch.

Im Wellington Magicians' Club zeigen (1) ______________ ihre unglaublichsten Tricks. Sie treten in Schulen, Kindergärten, (2) ______________ und (3) ______________ auf. Wenn man jünger als (4) ______________ ist, zahlt man (5) ______________, wenn man älter ist, (6) ______________. Darin sind die Kosten für (7) ______________ enthalten. Die Mitglieder treffen sich (8) ______________ im Monat.

Lösungen online
i9v8fb

Ziel 1: Ich kann Informationen über Neuseeland verstehen.

North Island and South Island

The two large islands of New Zealand are called North Island and South Island. On North Island there are three large volcanoes. Around them you can find lakes, mountains and beaches with black sand. The east coast of North Island has many long beaches with golden sand.
North Island is smaller than South Island but it has the largest cities, for example Wellington and Auckland. Most of New Zealand's population live there.
South Island is larger than North Island. It has huge lakes, rivers, glaciers and beautiful beaches. The island also has many national parks. On both islands there are big sheep farms. There are about 27 million sheep in New Zealand but only about 4.7 million people.

Read the statements. There is one mistake in each sentence. Cross it out and correct it.

1. South Island is smaller than North Island. ______
2. You can find beaches with black sand around the cities. ______
3. There's golden sand on the beaches of North Island's west coast. ______
4. Most people live in small cities like Auckland on North Island. ______
5. There are national beaches on South Island. ______
6. There are about 27 million people in New Zealand. ______

Ziel 2: Ich kann über Jobmöglichkeiten und Fähigkeiten sprechen.

Put in the correct verbs.

is going to do | are going to work | am going to work | are going to ask | is going to be | are going to go | am going to send | are ... going to apply

Charlotte: Hi Matt. I (1) ______ as a receptionist after school. What about you?

Matt: Nick and I (2) ______ a careers advisor first. We (3) ______ to school again. Do you know what Ella (4) ______?

Charlotte: Yes, she (5) ______ a hairdresser. What about Cooper and George?

Matt: They (6) ______ at a garage. They love working with machines. Where (7) ______ you ______ for a job as a receptionist?

Charlotte: I (8) ______ my applications to some big hotels. I love big hotels.

○ ## Ziel 3: Ich kann einen Bericht über ein Praktikum schreiben.

Use these words to complete Fiona's report.

career | customers | days | own | internship | present | shelves | work

I was lucky. My uncle helped me to find an (1) ____________________ at a local fashion store. Last month I worked there for five (2) ____________________. I had to (3) ____________________ six hours every day. A shop assistant showed me how to (4) ____________________ the clothes nicely so that (5) ____________________ want to buy them. I also had to fill some of the (6) ____________________. I can say that the internship was quite important for my (7) ____________________. Maybe I'll have my (8) ____________________ fashion store one day.

○ ## Ziel 4: Ich kann eine Geschichte über verschiedene Generationen verstehen.

Read the Maori legend on page 66 again. Tick ✓ the right answer.

1. Uenuku built a boat for ...
   - ☐ a) the gods.
   - ☐ b) his sons.
   - ☐ c) Ruatapu's mother.
2. Ruatapu ...
   - ☐ a) didn't want to go on the boat.
   - ☐ b) sent a whale to his brothers.
   - ☐ c) cut a hole in the boat.
3. The lord of the sea saved ...
   - ☐ a) the great whale.
   - ☐ b) Paikea and his brothers.
   - ☐ c) Ruatapu.
4. Ruatapu himself was ...
   - ☐ a) not seen again.
   - ☐ b) happy in the end.
   - ☐ c) angry about Paikea.

○ ## Ziel 5: ich kann Informationen über einen Verein wiedergeben.

Welcome to the Wellington Magicians' Club (WMC)

Our evenings always start with a little show presented by our members.
- Experienced magicians show you some of their best tricks.
- There are lots of performances every year, for example at schools, in kindergartens, in hospitals and at birthday parties.
- Members under 20 pay a fee of NZ $25. Members over 20 pay NZ $35.
- The costs for the lessons are included.
- We meet once a month. Register now.

Unterstreiche im Text die Antworten auf die folgenden Fragen. Notiere Stichpunkte auf Deutsch.

1. Wer zeigt seine besten Tricks? ____________________
2. Wo treten die Zauberer auf? ____________________
   ____
3. Was zahlt man, wenn man jünger als 20 Jahre ist? ____________________
4. Wie oft treffen sich die Mitglieder? ____________________

Applying for an internship

Get work experience in a New Zealand kindergarten and improve your English.
Apply for an internship of 6–8 weeks.

You will ...
- work in a kindergarten in Wellington.
- help kindergarten teachers and children.
- take part in all activities.

You should ...
- like working with children.
- be communicative, flexible, reliable and friendly.

We offer ...
- good training in our kindergarten.
- nice guest families for your stay.
- English classes at your level.

Interested? Please contact
Charlotte Clark: xx@xxx.nz

1 Read the ad from New Zealand. Write an enquiry.

107/3

Use the enquiry (text 2) on page 106 in your book as a model. Look at the phrases on the right and use a dictionary if you need help.

Useful phrases for writing an enquiry
- Dear Mr/Mrs/Ms ...,
- I've read your ad about ...
- My name is ...
- I am interested in ... because ...
- I like working with ...
- I will finish school with a general school leaving certificate in ...
- Could you tell me more about ...?
- How often ...?/How many ...?
- I look forward to ... (verb+-ing)
- Yours sincerely, ... (your name)

E-MAIL

To: xx@xxx.nz
Subject: Your internship advertisement

Dear ____________________,

I've read your ad about ____________________

____________________. My name is ____________________, I'm ________

years old and I'm very interested in ____________________ because I like ____________________

____________________ and I would like to improve my ____________________.

I live in ____________________ and I will finish school with ____________________

____________________ in the summer. Could you tell me more about ____________________

____

How often ____________________ How many ____________________

____________________ I look forward to ____________________

Yours ____________________

____